R THE ARTIST—
75 7370

METALSMITHING

THE CRANBROOK PUNCH BOWL
By the Author, Sterling Silver, 24" diameter with the seals of the Cranbrook institutions centrifugally cast in sterling.   (Photograph by Harvey Croze)

RICHARD THOMAS

METALSMITHING
FOR THE ARTIST-CRAFTSMAN

CHILTON BOOK COMPANY
Radnor, Pennsylvania

Copyright © 1960 by Richard Thomas. First Edition. Third Printing. *All Rights Reserved.* Published in Radnor, Pa., by Chilton Book Company, and simultaneously in Ontario, Canada by Thomas Nelson & Sons, Ltd.

PHOTOGRAPH AND DRAWING CREDITS: Harvey Croze—illustrations I, II, IV, VI, Figures 1 through 4, 12 through 15, 17 through 31, 36 through 70, 72 through 74, 78 through 81, 83, 84, 115 through 182, 191 through 232, 243, 244, 245, 248 through 254, 257 through 273. All other illustrations, both photographs and drawings, by the author.

Library of Congress Catalog Card No. 60-14633
ISBN 0-8019-0465-X

Designed by William E. Lickfield, Manufactured in the United States of America

Fourth Printing, September 1974

FOREWORD

This book addresses itself to the task of illustrating and elaborating the materials and processes of metalsmithing. A perusal of the pages will reveal that this task has been achieved at a high level of technical proficiency and with a maximum of intelligent communication. Also revealed in the pages of this book is a good deal of the author's own character. Mr. Thomas here is making available not only his marked proficiency with the materials and techniques of metalsmithing, but also his understanding of the teaching of these. This book provides many insights which have grown out of years of dedicated and fruitful teaching. Further, it demonstrates clearly the historic and artistic grasp of the author. Mr. Thomas, with facility and imagination, seeks to share his understanding and knowledge with others, that their efforts to advance the important cause of art and art education in general and metalsmithing in particular will be reinforced significantly.

ZOLTAN SEPESHY

Cranbrook Academy of Art
Bloomfield Hills, Michigan
November 15, 1959

PREFACE

In the preparation of this book it has been my purpose to re-examine, re-evaluate, and re-define some of the skills and techniques that have survived to the middle decades of the twentieth century and that are significant to the individual small shop worker—student, practicing professional, or teacher—who is primarily concerned with unique or limited production and who is, essentially, a hand worker.

The range of necessary skills, knowledge, and information concerned with the working of metal is wide—almost unlimited if one includes the peripheral, complementing fields of engraving, carving, chasing, spinning, casting, die cutting, and toolmaking (which may be life occupations in themselves), enameling, nielloing, embossing, and other embellishing techniques, a knowledge of gem stones, exotic woods, ivory, and plastic, a familiarity with simple chemistry and alloy composition, an awareness of sources of supply, and an appreciation of use, care, and maintenance of power and hand tools. In addition, the contemporary metalsmith, governed by the ethical and mechanical principles selected by his predecessors, must exercise aesthetic and creative judgment. It has, therefore, been necessary for me to be selective in the general and particular parts of the total field.

The book is divided into four parts—forming, joining, surface treatment, and a final section containing general information applicable to the preceding parts.

I have purposely avoided delineation of end products, except where necessary to indicate the values of the process. I have used this device because of my firm belief that the successful design of an object is a personal achievement and that no one has the privilege of invading this mystic province.

In the discussions of the various processes I have tried to indicate alternatives because, here again, selection of the means by which an object is brought about is subject to individual requirement.

If this book has merit, the larger share of credit properly belongs to the craftsmen and craftswomen who are my student-colleagues of the Cranbrook Academy of Art.

RICHARD THOMAS

Cranbrook Academy of Art
Bloomfield Hills, Michigan

ACKNOWLEDGMENTS

In the preparation of any book a remarkably great portion of the work is contributed by others—freely and graciously. To my wife, Ruth, who typed the original manuscript; to Jane Ricketts, who typed the finished version; to Harvey Croze, who took most of the pictures; to Zoltan Sepeshy, who wrote the Foreword and permitted me the freedom of the metalsmithing facilities of the Cranbrook Academy of Art; and especially to my students over the years, I extend my thanks and gratitude.

RICHARD THOMAS

Bloomfield Hills
Michigan

CONTENTS

Foreword v
Preface vii
Acknowledgments ix

FORMING OF METALS

Chapter 1 3
   Raising 3
      Definition
      Body Mechanics
   Annealing 11
      The Process
      Pickle Bath
      Pickle Pans
      Testing Annealing
      Spot Annealing
   Measuring Sheet and Wire Stock 17
   Laying Out the Work 19

Chapter 2 22
   Raising 22
      The Process
      Dutch Raising
         The Process
      Angle Raising
         The Process
      Crimping
         The Process
      Pressing
         The Process
      Sandbag Method
         The Process
   Blocking 34
   Thickening the Edge 36
   Faults in Raising 36
   Repairing Edge Cracks . . . 37
   Checking the Work 38
   Raising Lead 39
      The Process

Chapter 3 43
   Forging 43
      The Process

CHAPTER 4 46
 The Hammers 46

CHAPTER 5 54
 The Tool and Its Use 54

CHAPTER 6 73
 Spinning 73
  The Process

CHAPTER 7 80
 Sand Casting 80
  The Process

CHAPTER 8 90
 Ingot Mold 90
  Ingot Mold—Casting

CHAPTER 9 92
 Centrifugal Casting 92
  The Process

JOINING OF METALS

CHAPTER 10 103
 Joining 103
  Definition
  Soldering
  Soldering Fluxes
   Common Solder
   Hard Solder
  Common Soldering
   Preparing the Work
   The Process

CHAPTER 11 112
 Hard Soldering 112
  Preparing the Work
  Jigs
  The Process

CHAPTER 12 118
 Riveting 118

SURFACE TREATMENT

Chapter 13 122
Surface Treatment 122
   Filing
      The File and Its Use
      The Process
   Hand-Worked Abrasives

Chapter 14 128
Buffing and Polishing 128
   The Tools
   The Compounds
   The Process

Chapter 15 131
Chemical Agents 131
   Cleaning
   Coloring

GENERAL SHOP INFORMATION

Chapter 16 137
Heating Devices 137
Hand Tools 138
Hand-Operated Machines . . . 140
Power Tools 140
   Drill Press
   Metal Lathe

DETAIL IN FINE CRAFTSMANSHIP   145
BIBLIOGRAPHY   169
INDEX   171

FORMING OF METALS

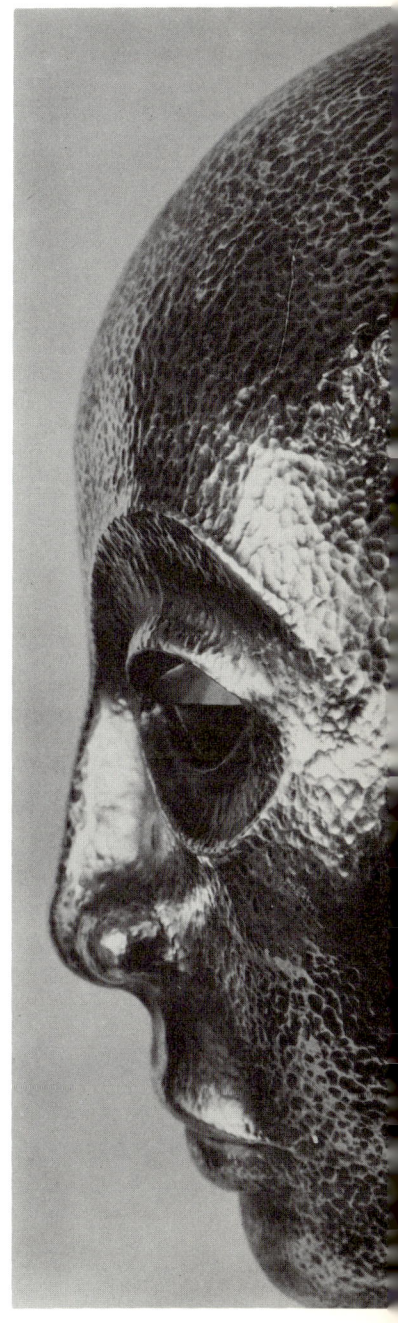

Detail of Raised Mask
By Rosemary Herkommer
Sterling Silver, 12″
(Photograph by the Author)

CHAPTER 1

RAISING

Definition

Raising is a hand-hammering process by which a sheet of flat metal may be formed into a seamless hollow vessel, ranging from an open shallow form to a hemisphere or a nearly closed sphere. Cylindrical, conical, or symmetrical and asymmetrical forms may also be made by this means. Raising is perhaps the most significant of the skills of the metalsmith, because the subtleties of form are here most personal and most defiant of duplication.

It is interesting to observe that most great historic cultures that tolerated metalsmiths among their artisans produced a local tradition of method that persists in contemporary hand raising techniques. These traditional methods vary only in detail, but the adherents of each are quite insistent about the advantage of their own special device.

In practice I have found at least six different ways that one may achieve, for example, a hemispheric shape. In combination these six methods may be extended to twelve or more distinct methods. The finished products have much in common and therefore suggest that any way that the worker uses to raise (or sink) a vessel is a valid way!

It would be well to explain the essential difference between raising and sinking. In raising, the work is started and continued through all stages on the outer or convex surface of the shape as it develops. (See Figure 1.)

Sinking differs from raising in that the work is directed to the inner or concave surface of the shape, as illustrated in Figures 2, 3, and 4.

A second important difference in the two methods, which must be taken into account in selecting the original sheet stock, has to do with thickness and diameter of the sheet. A raised vessel will require a relatively thin sheet of a diameter roughly equal to the depth plus the widest part of the projected shape. (See Figure 5.)

A sheet for sinking should be relatively thick because its original diameter does not change radically in process. (See Figure 6.)

When one uses a pressing technique, which will be discussed in detail later in this chapter, still a third variation exists. With this technique a heavy disklike slug of metal, which may be ¼" thick, may be used. The outer diameter will expand radically under repeated blows. (See Figure 7.)

Fig. 1.

Fig. 2.

In order to simplify the description of the various methods of making hollow vessels, from this point on, I will refer only to "raising," in the assumption that the reader will, by reason of the preceding definitions, be able to differentiate between the two variations.

Raising of metal depends upon the placement of the work in relation to the tool employed in such a manner that mechanical advantage is gained at the moment the pressure is delivered. There are several conditions under which this mechanical advantage or leverage may be achieved. (See Figures 8, 9, and 10.)

The first, and perhaps simplest, way is to provide a nonresisting or semi-resisting "backup" for the sheet metal, such as a shallow depression of lesser dimension than the sheet in a block of hard wood or a sandbag. The wood surrounding the depression supports the metal and leaves the part to be worked free to move under the blow. (See Figure 8.) With the sandbag the

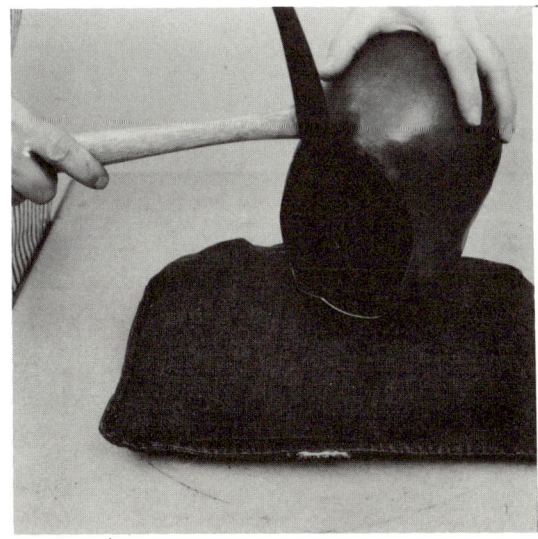

Fig. 3.

Fig. 4.

effect is essentially the same—the metal is uniformly supported, but the sand shifts aside directly under the blow and permits the metal to move. (See Figure 9.)

The second device which demonstrates mechanical advantage is a resisting surface, such as a hardened steel plate. When a blow is struck at the point of contact with the plate (see Figure 10), the metal is squeezed or pressed and flows outward from the blow.

The third advantage is achieved by striking the metal held at an angle against a steel surface and thus trapping the metal and forcing it in a new direction. (See Figure 11.)

A fourth possibility does not require backup, resisting, or nonresisting surfaces to act as local support or as a fulcrum against which the tool can exert its pressure, but merely takes advantage of the elastic quality of the metal itself. In this case the metal is suspended freely or held loosely in a frame, so that a blow can be delivered to the surface just as one would strike a drumhead. The difference between

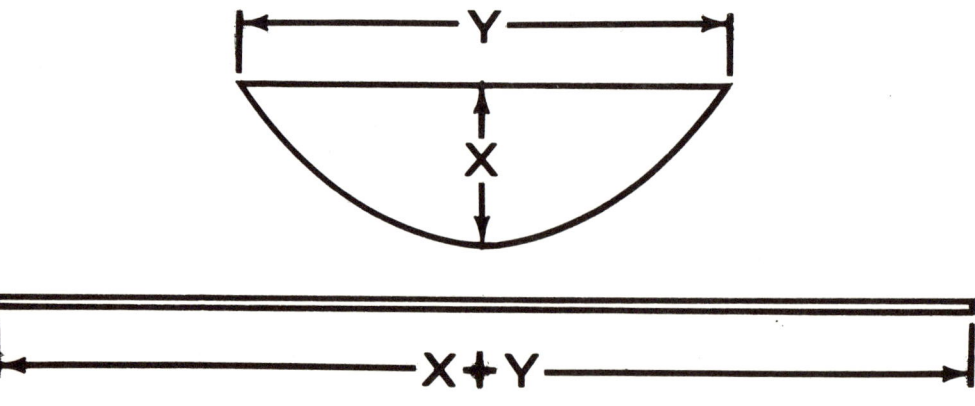

Fig. 5.

the drumhead and the suspended metal sheet is one of elasticity — the drumhead rides with the blow and because its limit of elasticity has not been reached, it returns to its original plane. The metal, unless it is very tough, hard, and resilient, will ride with the blow, stretch, and, because its limit of elasticity has been exceeded, does not return to its plane. It retains the dimple left by the hammer.

The latter method, which compares roughly with the metal spinner's "spinning in the air," is not used for small objects because of its obvious lack of mechanical advantage, but it may be used effectively for monumental sculptural forms, when the metal cannot, because of its size, be held conveniently by the worker and where the size and weight of the sheet offer sufficient resistance to the hammer.

As a matter of interest about "raising in the air," I understand that some workers who employ the method insist that the nature of the blow is so complex that one must spend years learning how it is done. This is, of course, ridiculous. The effect of the blow is

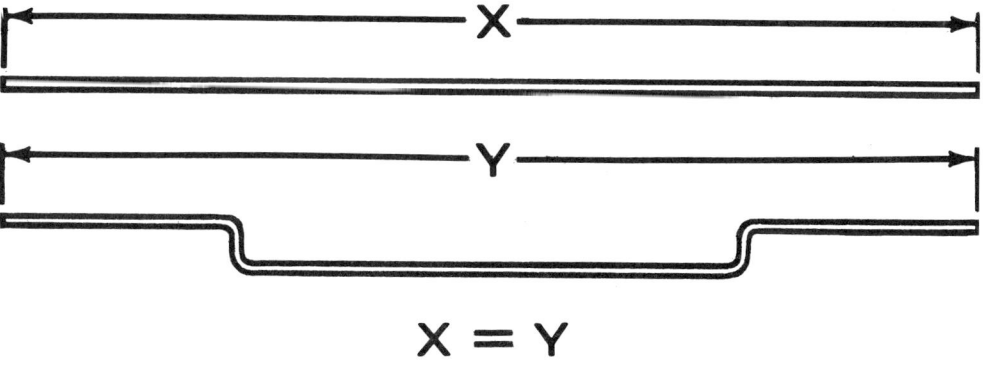

Fig. 6.

beyond revocation at the split second of contact with the metal. Any reasonably well-co-ordinated blacksmith with a minimal knowledge of his medium in five minutes can acquire the knack of selecting his tool, aligning his blow, and adjusting his muscular resources. If the adherents of the method are really speaking of form development — or even about handles with "whip" — that is another matter, but ascribing to a simple mechanical act such lofty potentials is without merit and does little to add dignity to the work.

Body Mechanics

I believe it necessary to alert the worker, particularly the beginner, with a brief discussion of body mechanics before he starts sustained raising. With the realization that as many as fifty thousand blows of varying pressure may be delivered to the metal with varying hammer weights (from a few ounces to 6 to 8 pounds), it becomes apparent that one must adjust his body to assume an easy, natural position in relation to the work, just as a polished athlete adopts a stance which

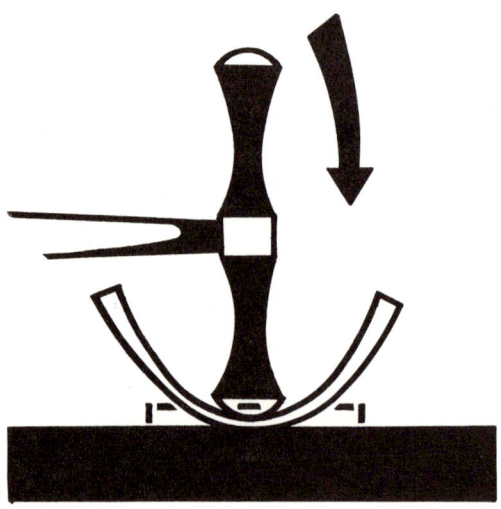

Fig. 7.

Fig. 8.

will assure maximum efficiency in his effort. Frequently I have seen students standing or sitting in positions utterly impossible for effective delivery of a blow. In such instances fatigue deprives the worker of the capacity for continued effort (so necessary for good work!) and the job becomes drudgery instead of the exhilarating experience it can be.

A very real danger of improper hammering procedure is the gradual development of a "tennis elbow" (a sprain of the *supinator brevis* muscle) — a distressing injury to the arm which manifests itself by causing difficulty in grasping objects. The injury is usually caused by crossing the working arm in front of the body, by raising the elbow away from the body, or by placing the work too high. At the first sign of pain in the elbow work should stop; the arm should be rested.

As a principle it is well to observe the following when work of long, sustained nature is begun: stand or sit with the work in line with working hand and shoulder, with the elbow close to the side. The work (the point

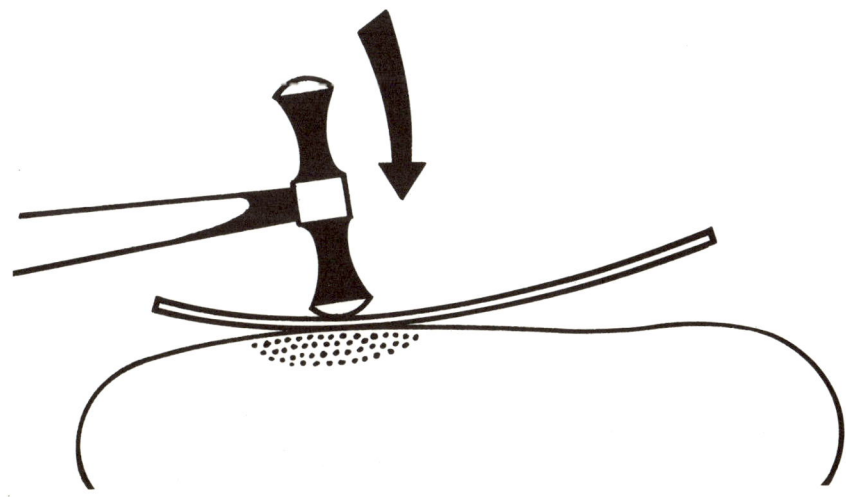

Fig. 9.

of contact with the hammer face) should be placed as close to the elbow level as possible. By loosely stiffening the wrist, the hammer head, handle, and forearm will swing as a unit; the power for the blow will then be delivered by the larger muscles of the upper arm, back, and chest. The hammer handle should be held at the extreme butt and the fingers should curl easily around it with a slight extension of the index finger. A simple way to assure a good grip is to adopt the practice of the tennis player—hold the hammer in the left or nonworking hand in a horizontal plane, work face to the floor, and "shake hands" with the handle.

In Figures 12 and 13 note that the hammer handle is parallel to and is an extension of the forearm at the beginning of the stroke and at the moment of impact with the work. The worker is standing with feet spread and with the body slightly turned to the stake, so that the left holding hand can comfortably shift the piece between blows.

The hammer handle should fit comfortably in the hand. If the handle is too large, it should be cut down with

FIG. 10.

a rasp and sanded smooth. Incidentally, I would not advise the use of tape or other coating on the wooden handle to improve the grip. Natural wood, well polished by use and preserved by the natural oils of the hand, is most satisfactory and should be cherished.

ANNEALING

Annealing is the process by which metal is subjected to heat to change it from a hard, springy state, induced by working — hammering, bending, forging, rolling, et cetera—to a soft, easily manipulated state.

Nearly everyone is familiar with the ease with which one may break an iron wire by rapidly bending it back and forth until the worked portion snaps like glass. This is the result of "work hardening."

Under work, metals undergo a structural change—a crystalline change. If this condition is not remedied at the proper time in the work process, further working will cause the metal

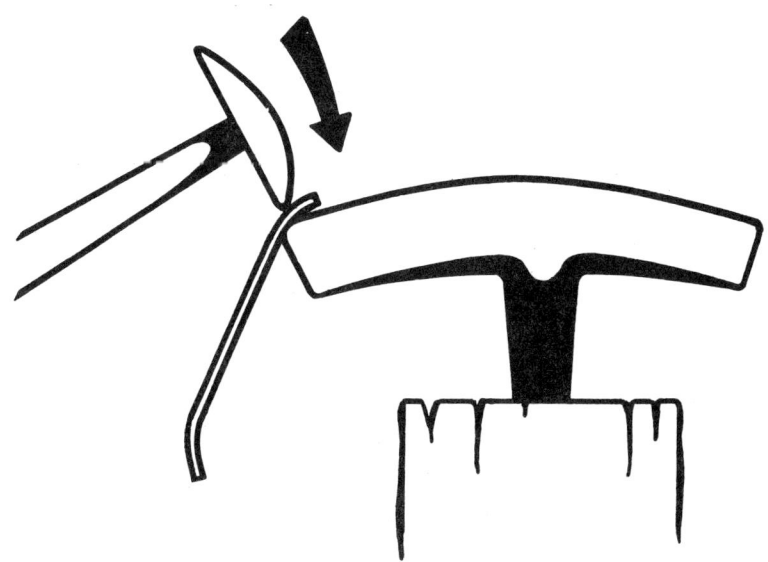

Fig. 11.

to crack or even shatter under a blow. The first indications of work hardening are easily recognized by the following signs: the effect of the blow is lessened; the sound of the blow, particularly when the metal is sandwiched between the hammer face and a steel stake, is sharper and of a higher pitch; and the surface of the metal near a worked part may take on an "orange peel" surface character. Of course, the ultimate sign of work hardening is a crack — a starlike crack in the body of the piece and hairline cracks at the edge. I will return to a discussion of the repair of such cracking later in this chapter.

If there is any doubt as to the condition of metal before starting work, annealing is desirable.

Fortunately, today the metalsmith may order his sheet stock in an annealed state, or, if he prefers, the stock may be ordered in half-hard or hard states.

The optimum annealing temperatures for the various elemental metals

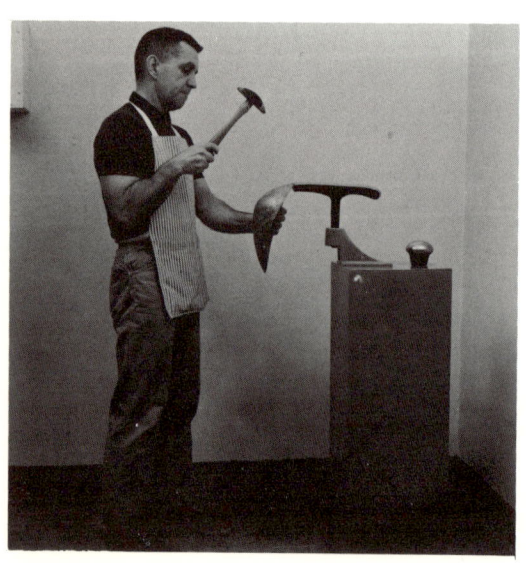

Fig. 12.

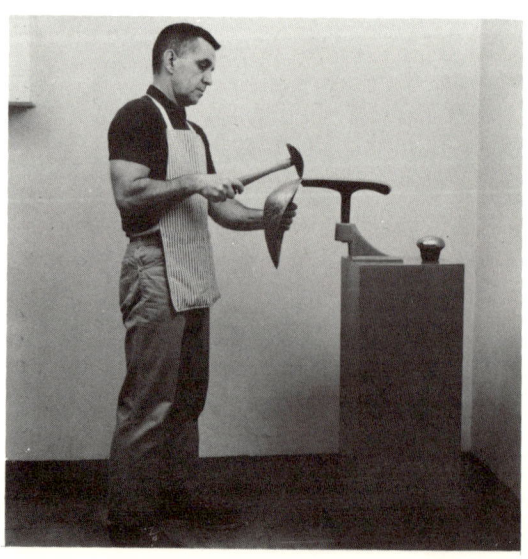

Fig. 13.

and their alloys have been determined, but this exact temperature is of little importance because color changes under heat are, in practice, the important key to proper procedures when the annealing is done in an annealing pan with an open flame, as is done in most small shops.

For the purposes of simplification this description of the annealing process will assume heating by open and direct air-gas flame rather than by furnace or muffle.

The Process

Clean the metal by abrasive or chemical means in order that scale from previous heats or marks left by the hammer do not interfere with observation of all parts of the surface.

Place the metal on the annealing pan well filled with rock pumice or other material not affected by heat. A rotating pan is useful because it permits the heat to be distributed uniformly over the entire surface of the metal. The room should be darkened.

Fig. 14.

Fig. 15.

Ideally, the annealing pan should be placed in a ventilating hood, away from uncontrolled natural light. (See Figure 14.)

Light and adjust the torch to a soft, feathery flame. Perhaps the simplest way to do this is to open the gas valve slightly and light the torch. Next, open the gas valve wide. This will produce a yellow flame, which indicates incomplete combustion. Then open the air valve until the yellow flame is replaced by a blue flame with a yellow tip. Reduce the gas until the yellow tips disappear. By further reducing the gas and balancing the flame with air, the flame may be shaped for greatest efficiency.

Direct the flame downward on the piece. If the torch is held at an angle to the piece, too much heat slips off and is lost. (See Figure 15.) The flame should be applied in a fanning motion.

At this point the color changes begin. The color changes vary slightly, depending upon the metal being annealed, but they generally follow the

Fig. 16.

same pattern and are much the same as those in a pigmental color sequence. The recognizable color sequence in the case of sterling is this:

1. Light yellow straw
2. Brownish-yellow straw
    Intermediate greenish trace
3. Blue
    Intermediate purple or magenta trace
4. Red — dull cherry
5. Red — red-orange
6. Red — yellow-red
7. Yellow
8. White

At the first red stage the metal takes on a glowing quality and, if the torch is quickly turned off, the metal will be faintly luminous in the dark.

The dull cherry red condition uniformly distributed over the surface indicates optimum heat, and it is at this point that annealing is complete. DO NOT raise the temperature beyond this point. Further heat serves no useful purpose and may result in destruction of the working quality of the material.

From time to time as you fan the flame over the surface of the metal, move the flame off to the side to check the color. With sterling, as you approach the proper annealing temperature, you can frequently observe a yellowish-green flame deflected off the surface. This is another indication that the heat is close to the annealing range.

When you are sure that the piece is uniformly annealed, remove the flame and turn off the torch. As a safety factor it is well to form the habit of

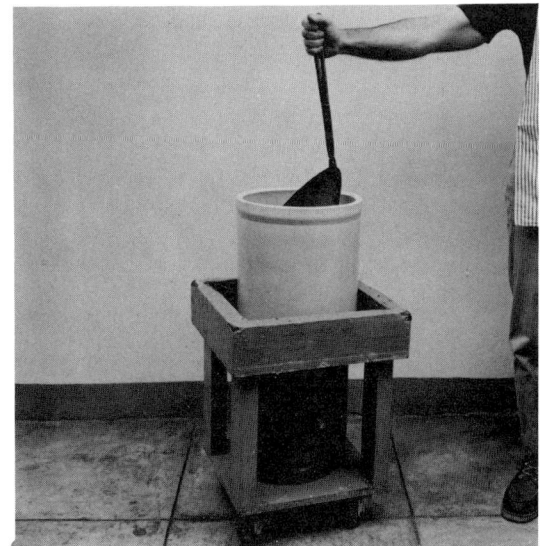

Fig. 17.

Fig. 18.

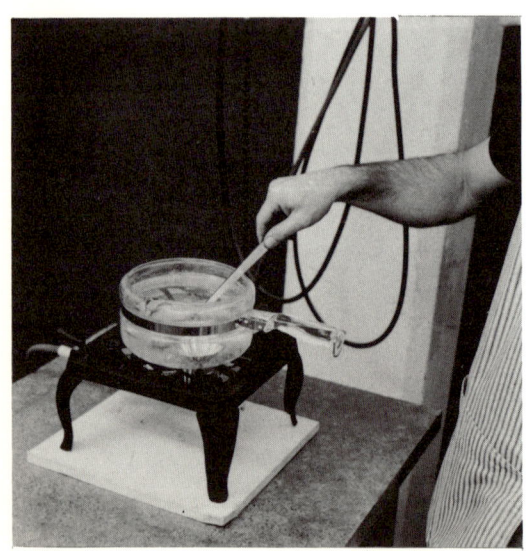

Fig. 19.

setting a definite sequence for torch operation. I prefer to follow this sequence: gas on; ignite gas; air on; adjust flame; air off; gas off.

Pickle Bath

With a pair of copper or bronze tongs remove the metal from the pan and quench it immediately in water or pickle. The pickle is preferable because it serves the dual function of quenching the piece and, because of the heat, of accelerating the removal of scale. The pickle bath is made up of sulphuric acid and water, in proportions of one part acid to six or eight parts water. The acid should always be poured into the larger volume of water. (See Figure 16.)

When you are introducing the hot metal into the pickle bath, stand well back because the spattering can quickly burn holes in clothing. The dilute acid is not particularly dangerous if it should spatter on your skin, but it should be rinsed off immediately. Of course, if the acid spatter should strike your eyes, rinse them immediately in running water and seek medical aid.

Pickle Pans

In some instances you may choose to accelerate the action of the acid by heating it. Hot pickle is particularly useful for removing flux residue and surface discoloration caused by annealing. In Figure 18, a heavy copper pot is shown on a gas hot plate. Figure 19 illustrates the use of a heat-resistant glass pickle pot.

Testing Annealing

It may be of interest to you to test the effectiveness of your annealing.

Take a hemisphere of about 16-gauge copper that has been thoroughly work hardened and try to flex it in your hands. Note its resistance. Now drop the hemisphere a short distance to a surface plate and note its sharp metallic ring. After annealing, repeat the process. You will find that the object may be twisted and bent easily and that the sound has changed from a sharp ringing one to a dull, dead clunk.

Spot Annealing

Although there are instances when spot annealing may be employed — as in the case of chasing and *repoussé* or when a boss is to be raised out of the side of a vessel — for the most part annealing implies uniform heating and cooling. If the object being raised is not "restructured," it becomes almost impossible to work effectively because hammer blows of equal pressure delivered to annealed parts and unannealed parts will most certainly have greater effect upon the softened parts and lesser effect on the hardened parts and thus will result in warping and twisting. The only remedy for inequities in the form (when the metal is of equal thickness throughout) is to stop working immediately and carefully anneal.

MEASURING SHEET AND WIRE STOCK

The metalsmith can gauge metal and wire thicknesses accurately with two simple devices — the American Standard Wire Gauge (Brown and Sharp Gauge) and the Standard Drill and Wire Gauge.

In Figure 20, the sheet of metal

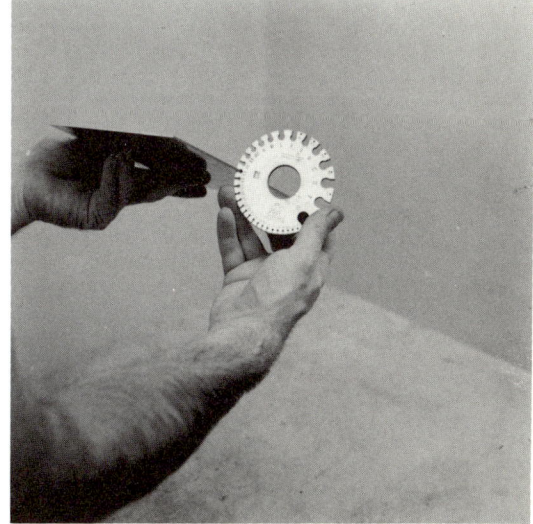

FIG. 20.

to be measured is shown inserted into one of the slots in the edge of the Standard Wire Gauge. When the metal slips snugly into the slot (it is well to measure the metal at several points to make certain that you are not measuring a burr!), read the number stamped on the surface of the disk directly in line with the slot. This number is the gauge size. The designation is usually written "14 gauge" (B & S) or "22 gauge" (B & S). High numbers indicate thin sheets; low numbers, thick sheets. The decimal equivalents to the number systems are stamped on the other side of the disk. The metal thicknesses normally used by the smith for raising purposes range from 8 gauge (B & S) for pressing through 20 gauge (B & S) for angle raising. The best thicknesses for general raising are 14, 16, and 18 gauge (B & S). Wire and rod stock are measured in the same manner. Only the slots around the perimeter of the disk are used for measuring. Don't use the holes!

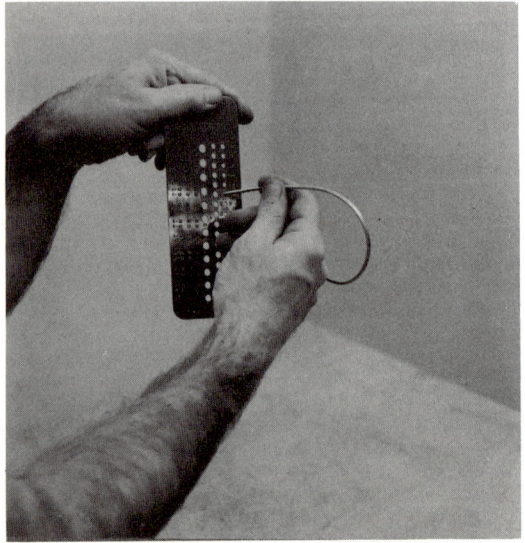

Fig. 21.

Fig. 22.

The Standard Drill and Wire Gauge is useful for determining the size of small twist drills ($\frac{1}{4}''$ and under) and for measuring wire to be inserted in drilled holes as may be required in riveting processes. This gauge and its use is illustrated in Figure 21.

LAYING OUT THE WORK

For the processes of raising, sinking, or spinning symmetrical forms, the preparation of the metal is much the same in each case and may follow this sequence:

1. Select the flat metal sheet stock of appropriate thickness and size. (For the illustrations in this book I have consistently used copper — 16 gauge or .051, the decimal equivalent to 16 gauge.) Clean the metal and inspect the surface for pits or deep scratches. If the surface is marred, remove the defect with abrasive papers or buff and polish out.

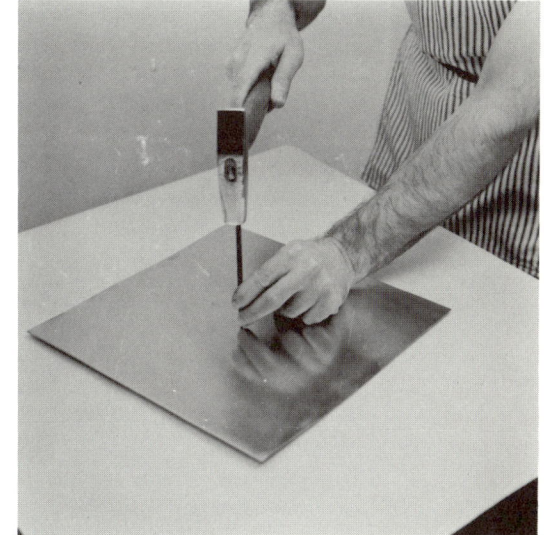

Fig. 24.

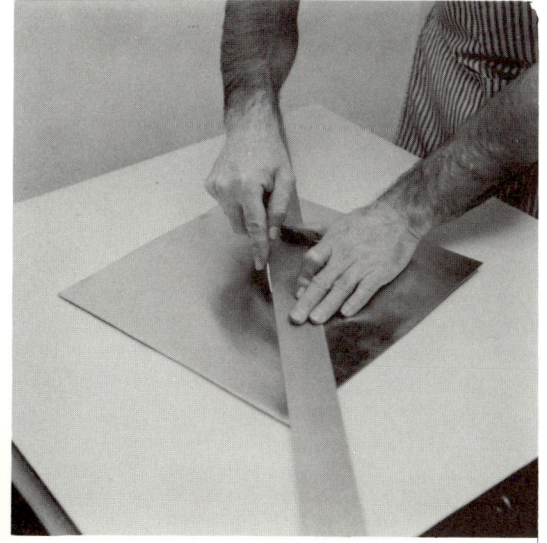

Fig. 23.

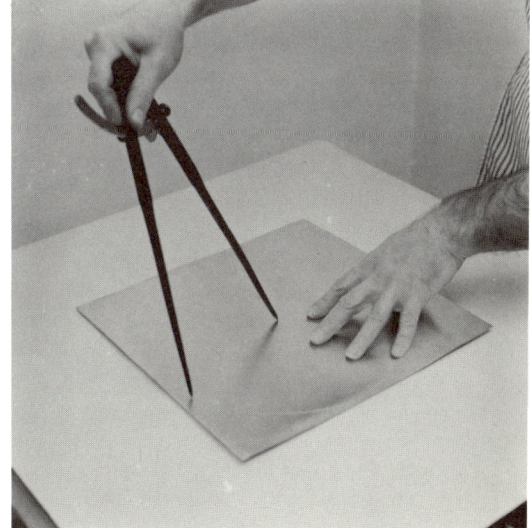

Fig. 25.

2. Lay a straightedge from corner to corner diagonally across the square sheet and scribe a line near the visual center. Repeat the process, using the opposing diagonal. (See Figures 22 and 23.) The intersecting lines will mark the center.
3. With a center punch locate the point of intersection of the lines and mark lightly by tapping the punch with a hammer. (See Figure 24.) This mark will be a useful reference point throughout the working process. In fine sterling holloware the center mark is not removed, and it has become almost a mark of authenticity.
4. With a set of dividers scribe a circle by seating one end

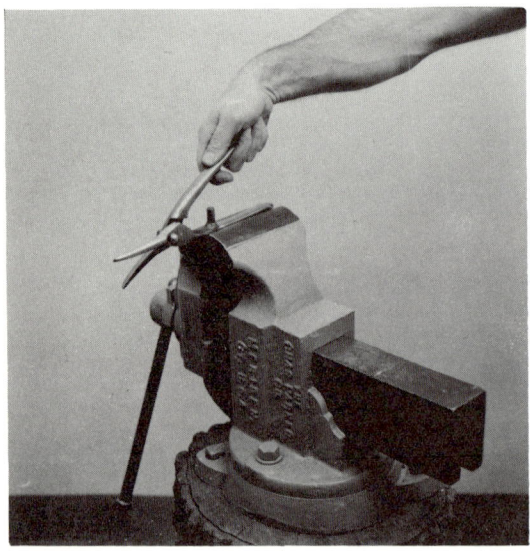

Fig. 26.

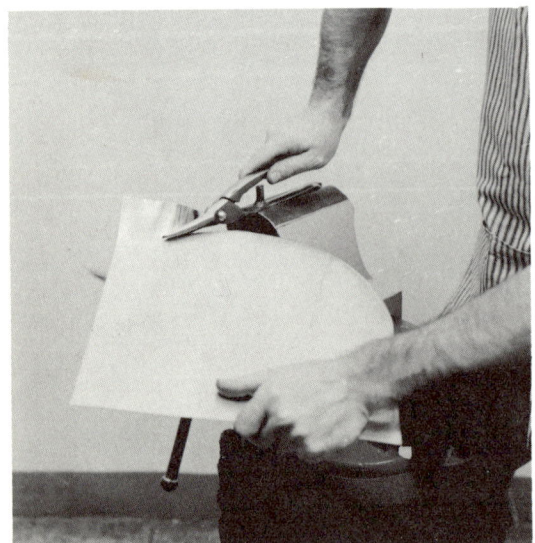

Fig. 27.

Fig. 28.

of the dividers in the center mark. (See Figure 25.)

5. The circle may be cut from the sheet by any means available to you. Figure 26 illustrates a pair of ducks-bill shears set in the jaws of a vise for greater mechanical advantage. Figure 27 illustrates the use of the shears in the vise.

Another useful mechanical device is the cutting head illustrated in Figure 28. This cutting head was removed from the bed of a ring-and-circle shear. Its use is demonstrated in Figure 29.

After the circle has been cut from the sheet, the edges should be carefully dressed to the line with a file. (In all cutting operations, the cut should be made so that the scribed line is not obliterated. It is needed for reference.) In Figures 30 and 31, two methods of holding the files are shown.

FIG. 30.

FIG. 31.

CHAPTER 2

RAISING

The Process

Dutch, angle, and crimping are all raising methods that require that the blows be directed to the outer or convex surface and that the metal be held at an angle against a stake. The effectiveness of the method is dependent upon the worker's awareness of a simple mechanical factor which may be explained by the following paragraphs and figures.

In Figure 32, assume that the horizontal line is a bar resting on a fulcrum, represented by the triangular solid shape. If one were to deliver a blow at point A, the bar would move to the position indicated by the broken line (A to C — B to D). No mechanical advantage would be gained. The reaction at B would equal the action at A. (There would be, of course, a friction factor to be considered, but that is not important for our purpose.)

In the second example, Figure 33, the fulcrum is moved off center. The blow at A produces a greater reaction at B. If the action were reversed, me-

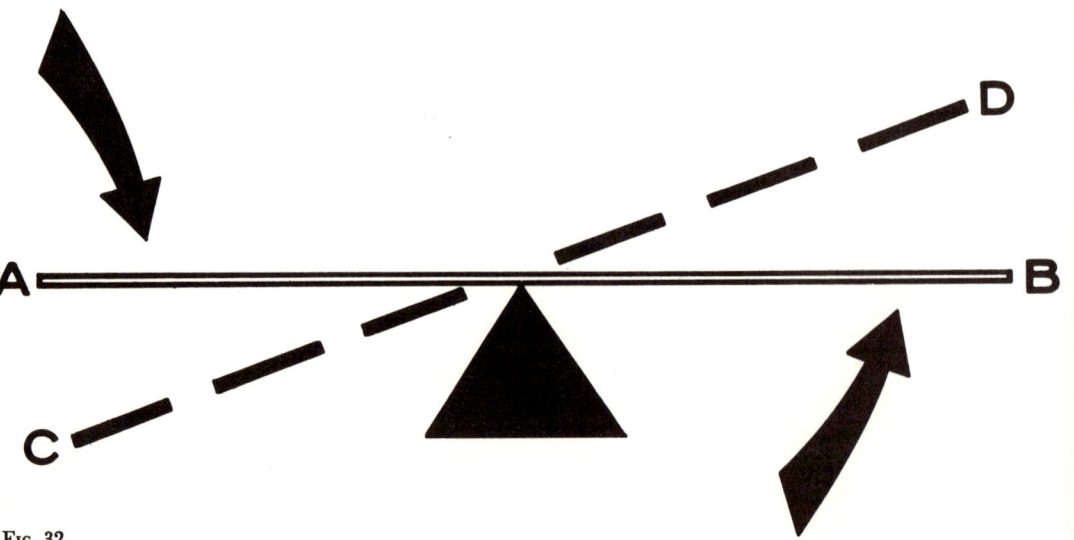

Fig. 32.

chanical advantage would be gained in rough proportion of five to two. If point B were held rigidly in place by some means and a heavy blow delivered at A, the bar would bend or break.

In the third diagram, Figure 34, the fulcrum is moved still farther off center and point B has a mechanical advantage over point A of roughly seven to one. If B were held in place, a blow at A would certainly bend or break the bar.

Now try to visualize the bar as a disk of metal, the fulcrum as the edge of a stake, the arrow indicating a hammer blow at A, and the hand holding the disk at B, as in Figure 35. It is upon this mechanical advantage factor that the effectiveness of true raising depends. This illustration also indicates why all work in raising must be done at the very edge of the stake.

Dutch Raising

THE PROCESS. Dutch raising is so called because of the craftsman who developed the process. The work is done by placing the metal disk at an

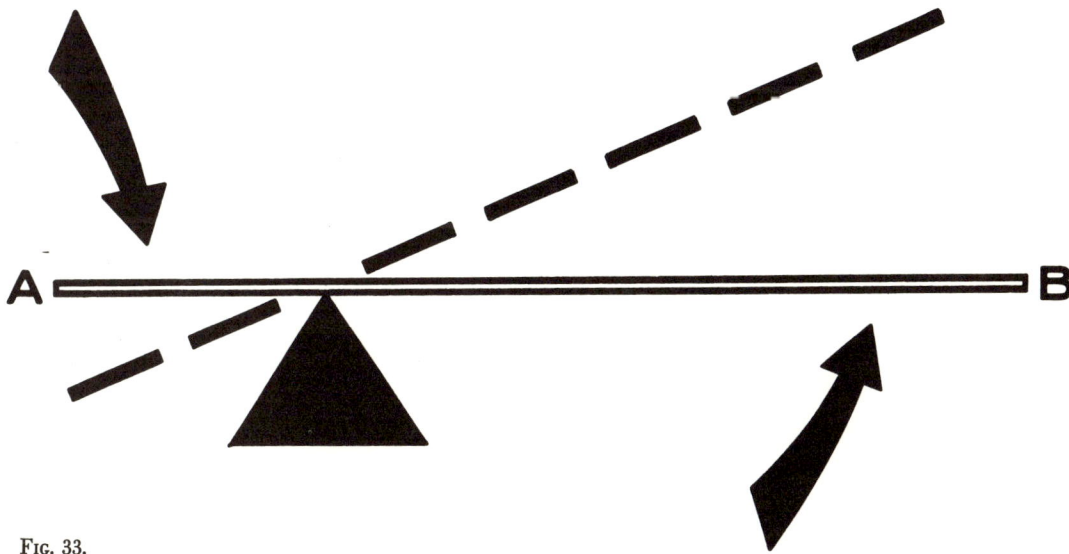

FIG. 33.

angle against the T-stake, striking the portion projecting above the stake, and driving it to the horizontal plane, as illustrated in Figure 36.

The work continues from the outer edge of the disk in an orderly sequence. In Figure 37, the angle is increased as the first series of blows are delivered to drive the metal at right angles to its original plane.

In Figure 38, the work is progressing toward the center of the piece. The hammer used is a cross-peen weighing 1½ pounds. The hammer is held at the butt for added leverage.

In Figure 39, a heavy rawhide mallet is employed to work out irregularities in the surface. The raised portion of the metal is held parallel to the horizontal surface of the stake.

With the cross-peen hammer the work is continued toward the center. Of course, annealing is necessary at various stages of the raising sequence. (Refer to section describing annealing.) (See Figure 40.)

The rawhide mallet is used frequently during the raising process. The

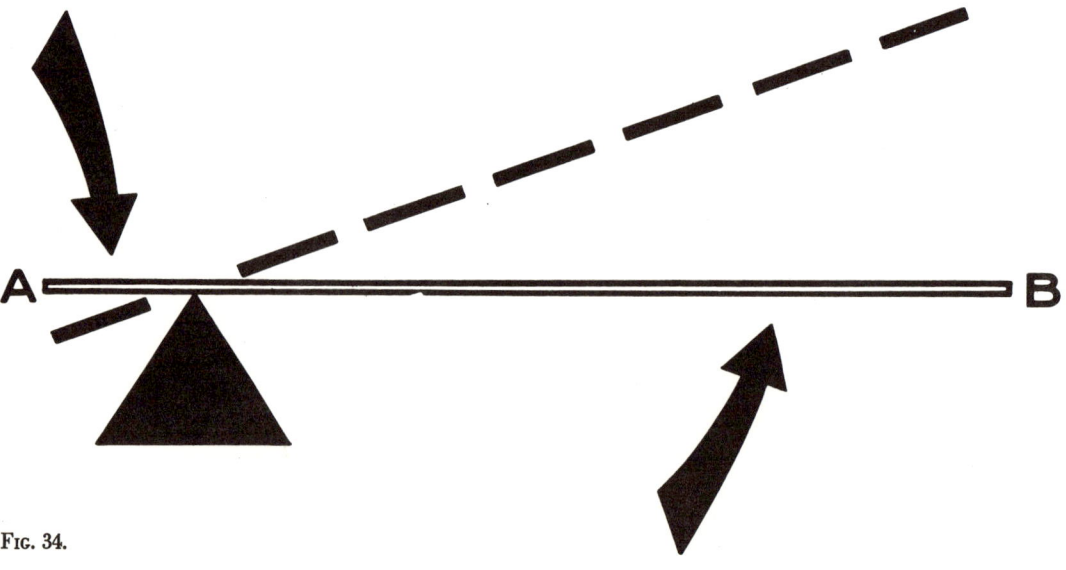

FIG. 34.

rough removal of surface irregularities by this means is called "bouging" —a word of French root meaning "moving." (In pronunciation it rhymes with "rouging.") (See Figure 41.)

In Figure 42, the center has been reached and the angles removed by working the piece over a mushroom vertical stake that has been substituted for the T-stake. Again the rawhide mallet is used. The piece should be annealed before this rough bouging process.

In Figure 43, the hemisphere is shown during the planishing stage. Planishing is done with a light, flat, or slightly dome-faced hammer. Its purpose is to remove all surface irregularities. This is the tool that leaves the characteristic mark of the hand hammered vessel.

Angle Raising

Angle raising is a true raising method that gets its name from a series of angles built up in the process. It is very similar to Dutch raising in that the metal disk is held at an angle against the T-stake and the work is accomplished by trapping the metal between the hammer face and the stake surface. But rather than working from the outer edge to the center of the disk, the progression is reversed.

THE PROCESS. The metal is prepared as previously described. From the center mark, scribe a circle about 2″ in diameter. This line will mark

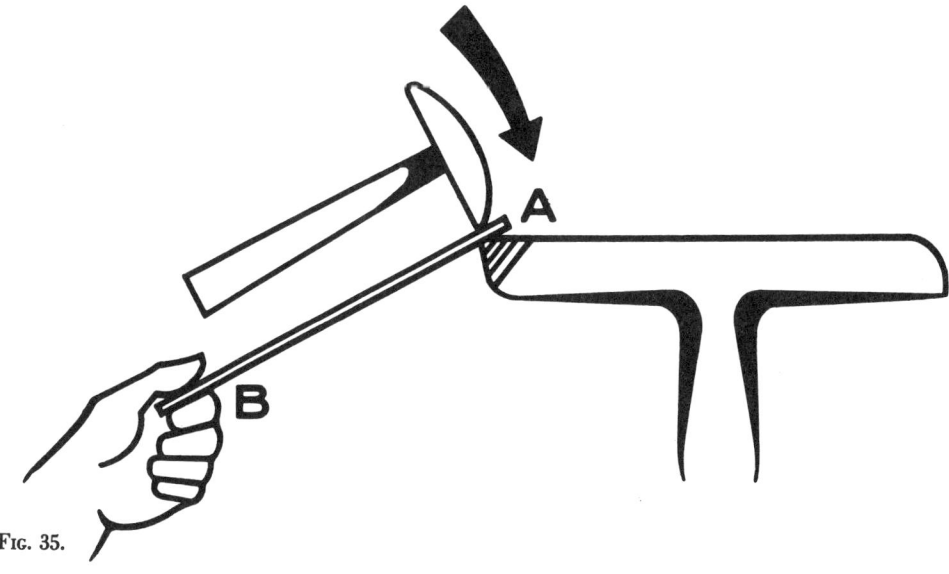

FIG. 35.

Fig. 36.

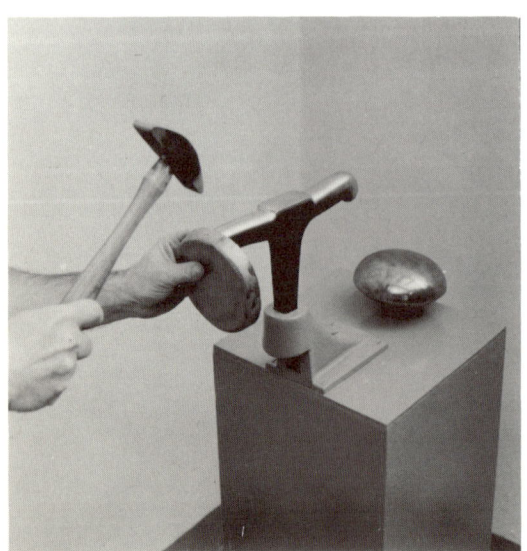

Fig. 37.

the beginning of the first course of the first angle. (The "course" is a term which is applied to a complete cycle of hammering, bouging, and annealing stages.) Lay the metal against the stake at about a 45° angle at the scribed line and strike just above the point of contact with a cross-peen hammer. Continue the blows and rotate the disk with the holding hand until the outer edge is reached. Do not strike the metal at the very edge; hold back about $\frac{1}{4}''$. (See Figure 44.)

In Figure 45, the second course of the first angle is nearing completion. The angle at which the metal is held has been increased slightly to increase the raised angle. The metal is, of course, annealed before each new angle is started.

In Figure 46, the third course of the first angle is nearly completed. The cross-peen raising hammer used in this sequence is a relatively light one—12 ounces—selected because the blow required is not a driving one.

After annealing, the first course of

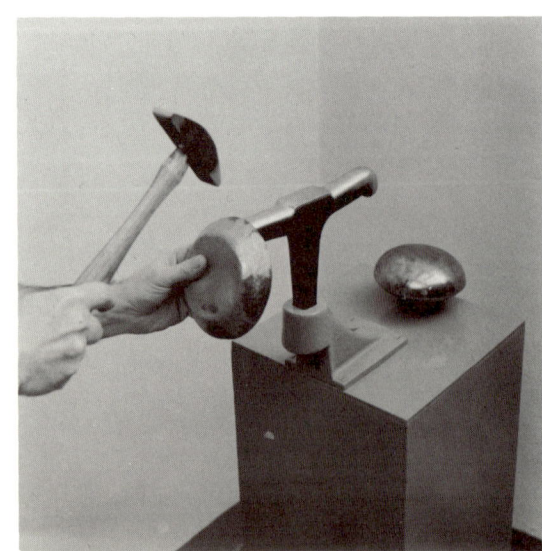

Fig. 38.

the second angle is started about ½″ above the original scribed line. Again, the angle at which the metal is held against the stake is increased slightly and the new course continued just short of the outer edge. (See Figure 47.)

The piece is annealed, and the first course of the third angle is struck off. In this case the third angle was started at a point between the second angle and the outer edge. (See Figure 48.)

In Figure 49, the second course of the third angle is being completed. The number of courses for each angle will vary considerably. Some highly skilled craftsmen will require only two courses. The beginning may require six!

After the angles have been completed, they are worked out by bouging with a heavy rawhide mallet. A mushroom vertical stake has been substituted for the T-stake for this purpose. (See Figure 50.)

In Figure 51, the raised hemisphere is refining by planishing out all traces

Fig. 40.

Fig. 39.

Fig. 41.

of the angles and the marks of the cross-peen hammer. A mushroom vertical stake conforming roughly to the interior contour is used to back up the planishing hammer.

Crimping

Raising by crimping is a radical departure from the two methods previously described in that the metal is deliberately distorted at several stages. For this reason, though admittedly effective, the technique is particularly difficult for the inexperienced.

Crimping is frequently used in conjunction with other raising sequences because it has the advantage of rapid angle change. The method requires a special stake form—the valley stake, which is illustrated in the first stage of the raising sequence. A better definition of the valley stake will be found in the chapter on "The Tool and Its Use."

THE PROCESS. The prepared disk is laid across the valley stake, and with a rounded cross-peen hammer the

FIG. 42.

FIG. 43.

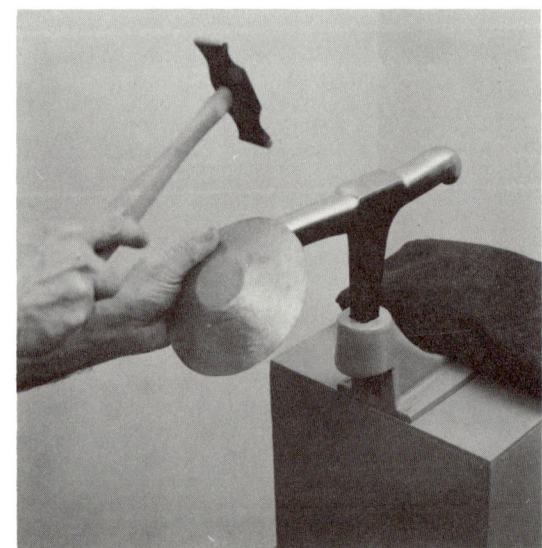

FIG. 44.

metal is driven into the groove with several sharp blows. Rotate the disk and make grooves extending from the center to the outer edge all the way around, as illustrated in Figure 52.

After the grooves have been placed uniformly, anneal the disk and place it at an angle of 45° against the working edge of a T-stake at a line about 2" from the center. With a cross-peen hammer of good weight (1½ pounds) remove the grooves by trapping the metal between the hammer and the stake. Work from the inside out. Figure 53 illustrates this stage nearly completed.

Anneal the piece and again sink the grooves by driving the metal into the valley stake, as shown in Figure 54. Many craftsmen prefer to drive the valleys from the outer or convex side. Either way will work well.

Again the T-stake replaces the valley stake, and with the cross-peen the grooves radiating from the center are removed. As illustrated in Figure 55, the angle of the raise is increased as

FIG. 46.

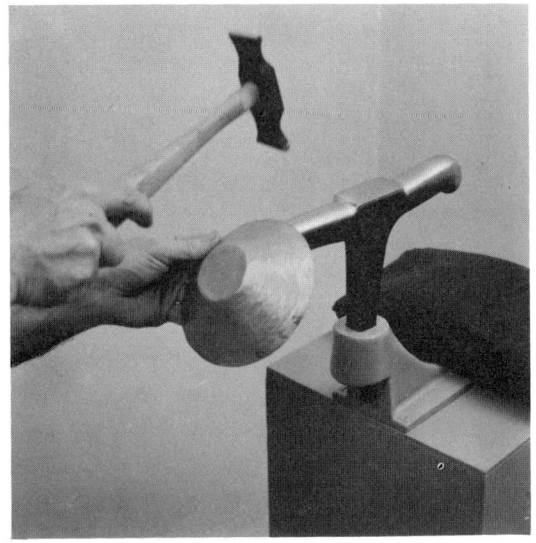

FIG. 45.

FIG. 47.

the angle at which the metal is held against the stake is increased.

To check the form, it is well in all raising sequences to bouge the piece. In Figure 56, the surface irregularities are being removed with a heavy rawhide mallet backed up by the horizontal surface of the T-stake.

In Figure 57, the final set of valleys or grooves are driven into the raised form.

The final cross-peening of the metal is nearing completion in Figure 58.

After the final bouging for removal of surface defects (see Figure 59), the piece may be planished over a conforming stake, or the angle may be worked out after annealing by bouging carefully over the rounded end of the T-stake and the whole piece finished as a hemisphere like those described in previous raising sequences.

Pressing

Pressing (also called "stretching") is probably the oldest method of raising metals because it may be started

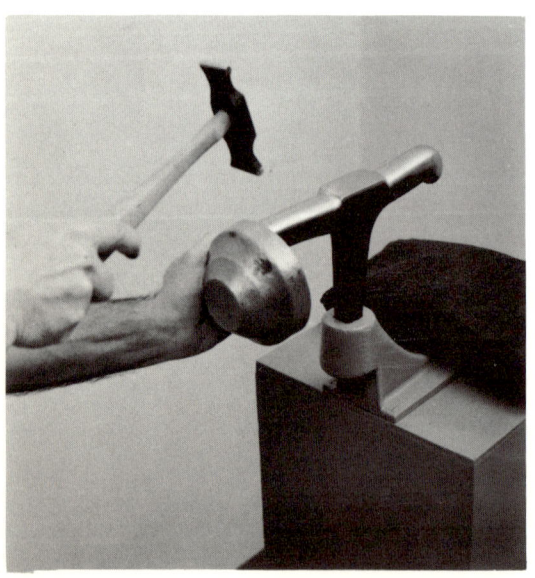

Fig. 48.

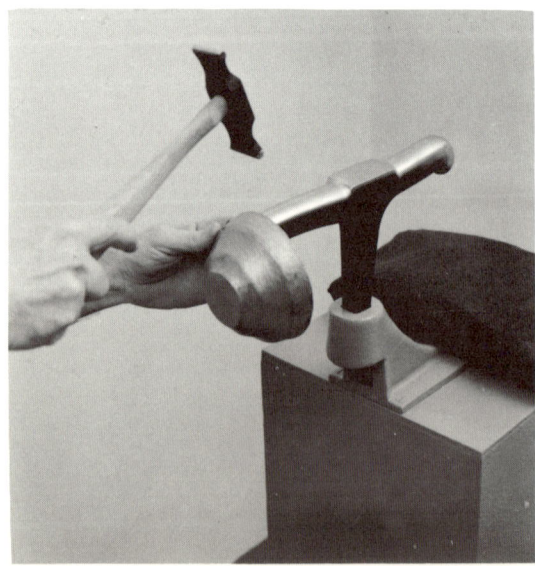

Fig. 49.

from a thick slug of metal roughly poured directly from the crucible. In contemporary practice a disk ranging from $\frac{1}{8}''$ to $\frac{1}{4}''$ in thickness may be used. Obviously, a tenacious metal should be used for pressing, because it is subject to considerable pressure. While a heavy disk is desirable, thinner sections may be used. In this series of illustrations 12 gauge (B & S) copper is used.

THE PROCESS. Place the metal on a steel surface plate or, as illustrated in Figure 60, on the center portion of a heavy T-stake. Starting in the center, strike a blow and follow it with succeeding ones spiraling outward to just short of the edge.

After annealing, repeat the process, as illustrated in Figure 61. The hammer weight and shape are particularly important for pressing. In this group of illustrations the tool is a heavy, dome-faced embossing hammer weighing $2\frac{1}{2}$ pounds.

In Figure 62, the hammer is shown in contact with the metal, which is

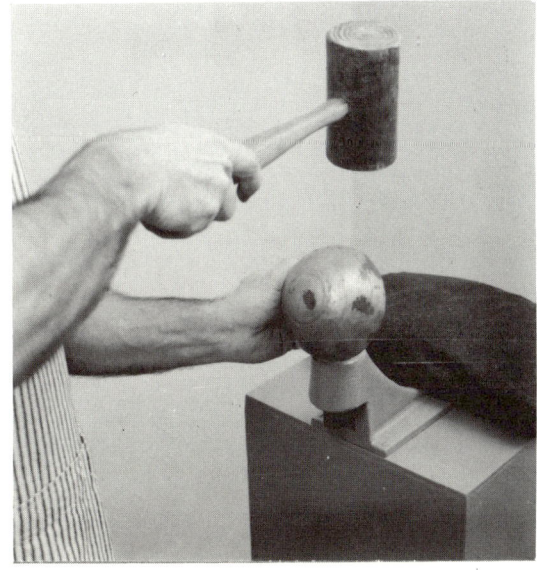

FIG. 50.

FIG. 51.

sandwiched between the resisting surface of the stake and the dome of the hammer face. All action takes place at this moment of impact.

The pressed shape is nearing completion in Figure 63. Frequent annealing, decisive and massive hammer blows, and sound co-ordination between the left or holding hand and the working hand are especially important in pressing.

In Figure 64, a vertical stake is substituted for the T-stake. The vessel is bouged and planished in the manner described previously.

Sandbag Method

This method is the simplest method of raising an open shape because it is direct—one can easily see the shape growing—and because using the tools employed requires no special skill. It must be remembered, however, that this is really a "sinking" process and the metal is stretched to make the shape. The original circumference of the disk is not changed appreciably.

Fig. 52.

Fig. 53.

Fig. 54.

THE PROCESS. Place the prepared disk with the center mark down on the bag. The bag is usually made of tough canvas filled with coarse sand. It is helpful to add oil to the sand to keep the dust down. Strike the center of the disk with a heavy embossing hammer and spiral succeeding blows short of the edge, as illustrated in Figure 65.

The first few blows will probably wrinkle the metal badly. When this happens, anneal the metal and work the wrinkle out over a vertical stake with a rawhide mallet. (See Figure 66.)

In Figure 67, the work (the second course) is continued. The hammer shown in Figure 67 is a relatively flat-faced embossing type weighing $2\frac{1}{2}$ pounds.

The hammering portion of the third course is illustrated in Figure 68. Here too one must be aware of the necessity for co-ordination between the holding hand and the working hand.

In Figure 69, the final bouging portion of the third course is illustrated. This will remove gross surface irregu-

FIG. 55.

FIG. 56.

larities and prepare the piece for planishing.

Planishing is started in the center. The blows overlap one another as they progress to the outer edge. In Figure 70, the first planishing is nearly completed. You may choose to planish several times.

BLOCKING

As a preliminary stage to many raising processes, the edge of the metal disk may be broken or "blocked" by driving it into a shallow depression in the end of a stump. (See Figure 71.) While blocking is useful, it is rarely used as a raising process in itself. I would urge the aspiring smith to avoid the use of fixed forms such as those cut into wooden or steel plates. These forms rob the artisan of the opportunity to devise his own shapes. In Figure 72, the method of blocking is shown. The stump is hard maple; the metal, a 12″ disk of 14-gauge copper; the hammer, a 1½-pound embossing type with a full dome face.

Fig. 57.

Fig. 58.

Fig. 59.

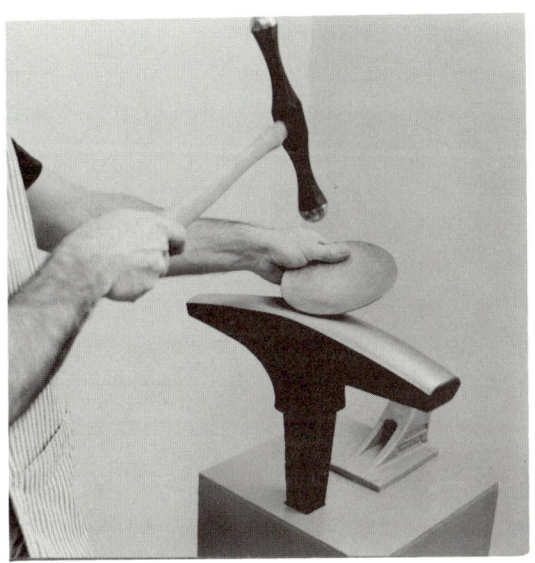

Fig. 60.

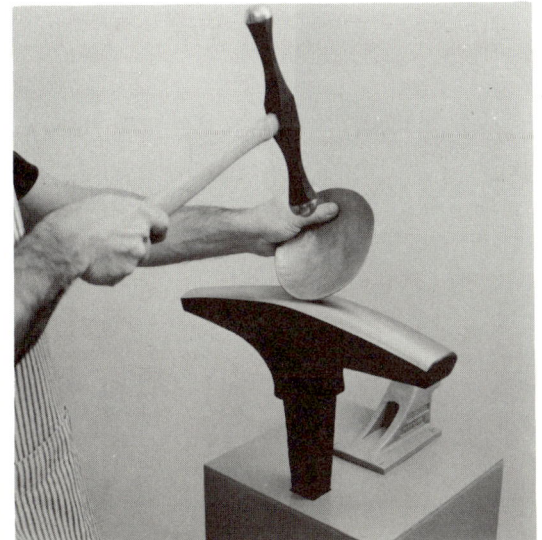

Fig. 61.

Fig. 62.

Fig. 63.

Fig. 64.

Fig. 65.

THICKENING THE EDGE

The edge of a raised vessel may require thickening to resist stress. This may be done during all of the raising processes previously described by upsetting the edge with a light collet hammer, as illustrated in Figure 73. This is not a single operation, but one that must be incorporated in each course sequence (annealing, raising, bouging). The work may be best accomplished by holding the vessel in a sandbag and striking the edge with light overlapping blows immediately after the bouging stage in the course sequence. The number of edge-thickening stages will then equal the number of courses required to raise the piece. Care must be taken that the delivered blows not be too heavy; a wire or rolled edge would result. The hammer must be held so that the long axis of the working face is at right angles to the edge being worked.

FAULTS IN RAISING

Common faults in the raising process result from two main deviations from sound practice—inequity in distribution of blows and spotty annealing.

The first error may be corrected by marking concentric circles with a compass about ½″ apart from the center to the perimeter of the form and then striking lines with a flexible rule across the convex surface dividing the surface into equally marked sections between the concentric circles. (See Figure 74.)

Then, starting in the center, deliver a series of blows in a rhythmic manner (most workers strike three or five blows before pausing to shift the object to bring it into proper contact with the stake, sandbag, or depression) and count the number of times the hammer has struck the defined space. In a short time, by unconsciously counting the blows and placing the same number of blows (equal pressure) in each like space, it will be found that symmetrical development of the form will come about.

In the case of an asymmetric form you may mark the piece in the same manner except that the initial lines should "contour" the object in exactly the same manner as a contour map delineates land elevations. (See Figure 75.) The radiating lines then would be struck from the several high points.

REPAIRING EDGE CRACKS

Figure 76 illustrates a method of repairing cracks in the edge of a raised vessel. The procedure: Find the end of the crack and mark it for drilling with a center punch. Drill the hole and insert a wire or rod of a slightly smaller dimension, so that it fits snugly. The

Fig. 67.

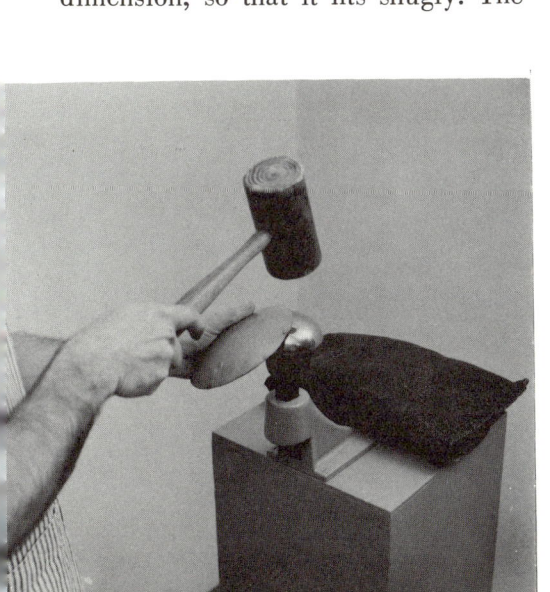
Fig. 66.

Fig. 68.

wire or rod should, of course, be of the same material as the parent body. Cut off the wire and leave it protruding on the outside of the vessel and flush on the inside. Clean and flux the crack and the pin. Flow hard solder under heat around the pin through the joint. Capillary action will draw the solder into place. Clean the soldered piece in pickle and file off the excess solder and the protruding pin. After buffing and polishing the join will show slightly, but this is better than a crack!

CHECKING THE WORK

In order to make certain that a raised object is conforming to plan, it becomes necessary to resort to some mechanical device for checking the work rather than to depend upon visual inspection of the piece in progress.

In that section of this book in which the preparation of the metal for raising is described, the value of an accurate center mark was stressed. Now the retained center mark in the nearly completed vessel again becomes use-

Fig. 69.

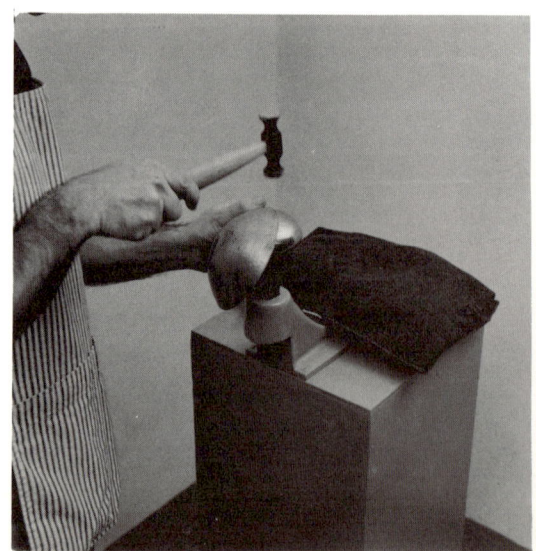

Fig. 70.

ful. In Figure 77, one point of a set of curved dividers is seated in the center mark; the other end, swinging from the point, is being used to scribe a light line completely around the vessel at some point on the side.

Now center the vessel on a turntable and rotate it lightly against the point of a surface gauge, as illustrated in Figure 78. If the two scribed lines —one struck off from the center point and one struck from the surface gauge —are parallel, the piece is sound.

RAISING LEAD

Lead is a fascinating material to work because of its remarkable plastic qualities, the ease with which it may be worked, its color, and its stability. For the craftsman, lead forms, of course, should be sculptural rather than functional in character, because the metal is poisonous and can cause serious harm if it is absorbed by the body. When working with lead, one should wash his hands frequently and avoid breathing in fine particles which

Fig. 72.

Fig. 71.

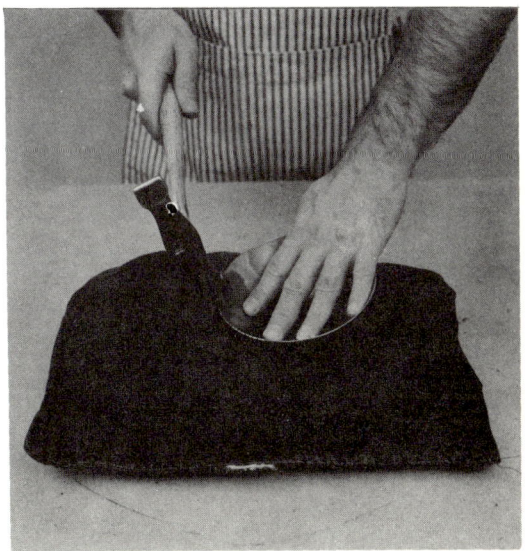

Fig. 73.

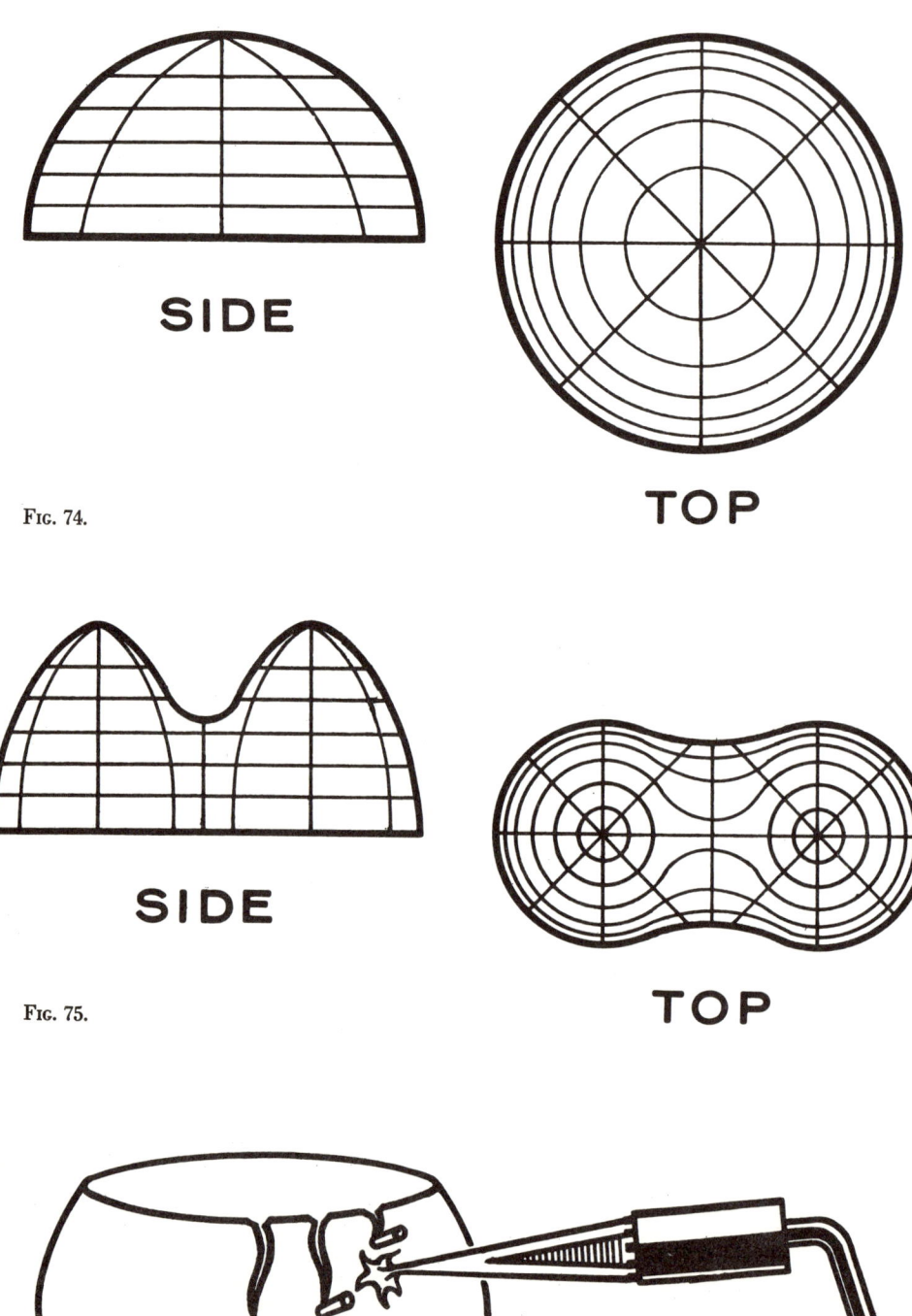

Fig. 74.

Fig. 75.

Fig. 76.

may arise during filing and abrading operations.

The Process

Although lead may be raised by any of the processes previously described, it is best to devise special broad-faced hammers of wood. One such hammer, an egg-shaped hard maple one, illustrated in Figure 79, was turned from an old bowling pin and fitted with a handle. The lead, $\frac{1}{8}''$ thick and 1' square, is shown being beaten on a sandbag.

In Figure 80, the lead is supported in the hand while the hammer blows drive the metal. This is useful because the holding hand can feel the precise effect of the blow and so can direct the worker in distributing equal pressures over the surface. Lead need not be annealed. It does not work harden appreciably.

Because lead is soft and presents, in itself, no great structural resistance to knocks and bumps, it must be backed up unless it is very thick. The hollow

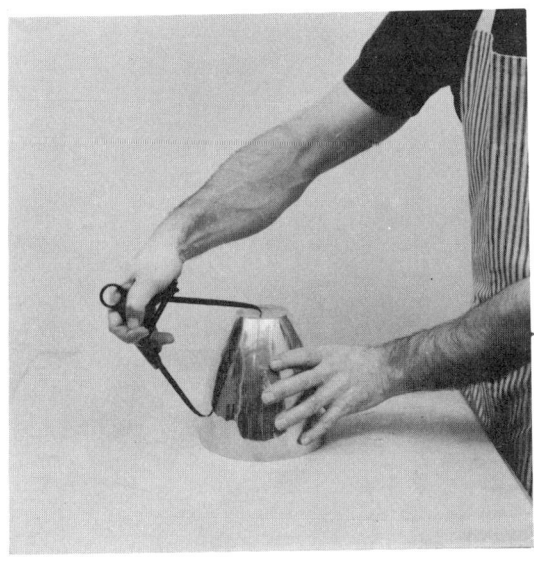

Fig. 77.

Fig. 78.

form may be filled with plaster to serve this purpose and to permit surface detail to be chased in, as Figure 81.

Figure 82 effectively demonstrates the subtle nature of lead as a sculptural medium. (This "Portrait of a Young Girl" was raised by Angelo Caravaglia and is in the permanent collection in the galleries of the Cranbrook Academy of Art.) It was raised from a sheet of lead $\frac{1}{8}''$ x 12" x 18".

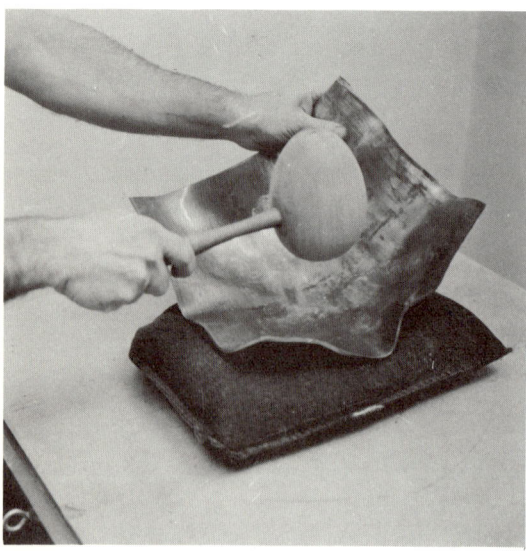

Fig. 79.

Fig. 81.

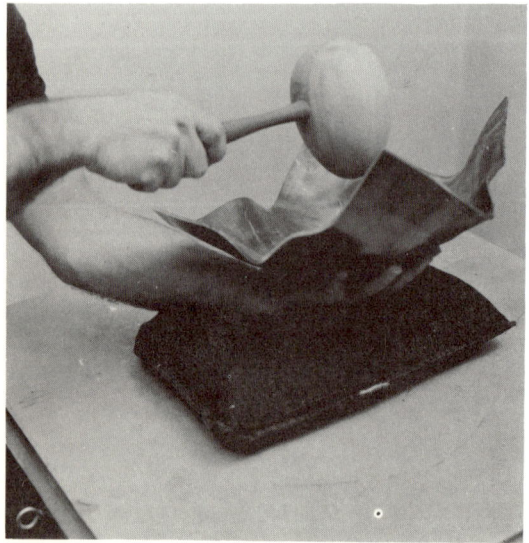

Fig. 80.

Fig. 82.

FORGING

Forging for the hand worker is a method of working metals by massive hammer blows (of course, with gold or silver, one may use the process with great delicacy!) which compress, elongate, twist, or distort the mass. Iron and steel are normally forged in the hot state, but nonferrous metals and alloys are worked cold after uniform annealing. Forging offers grace and flexibility of form difficult to achieve by any other means. For this reason, and for a genuine appreciation of the plastic qualities of metal as a working medium, every metalworker should acquire the skill.

The Process

In the sequence described here, a commercial bronze square rod, $\frac{1}{4}''$ in section, was used. A polished-steel surface plate mounted on an anvil was used as the resistant working surface.

In Figure 83, the metal held in the left hand is beaten with a $1\frac{1}{2}$-pound cross-peen hammer. The metal will, as

CHAPTER 3

Fig. 83.

shown, flow at right angles to the main axis of the hammer face.

After annealing, the work is continued as before, as illustrated in Figure 84. It is of particular importance that the metal be in contact, at the point of the blow, with the surface plate. This will increase control by eliminating "bounce."

A $6\frac{1}{2}$-pound dome-faced forging hammer may be used, as shown in Figure 85. The hammer weight is sufficient in itself to do the work of smoothing out surface irregularities left by the cross-peen. The dome-face will work the metal in all directions from the point of impact.

Figure 86 illustrates the use of the cross-peen hammer in elongating the metal slug. Remember that the metal flows at right angles to the long axis of the cross-peen hammer.

In Figure 87, the edge of the previously elongated length of metal is being thickened. This process, called "upsetting," restores the original

Fig. 84.

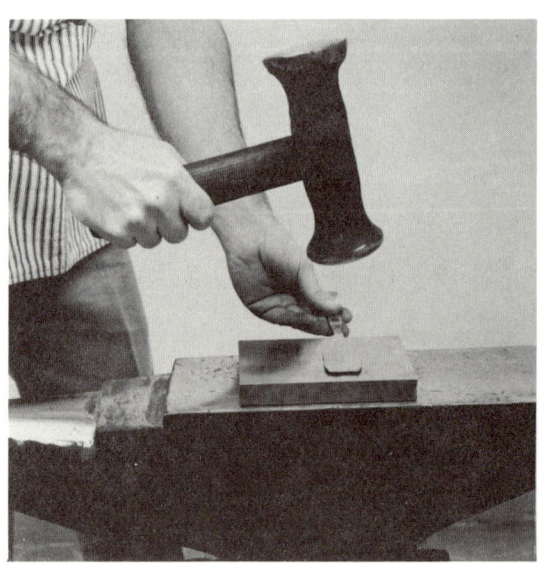

Fig. 85.

square section of the piece, though of lesser dimension.

The flowing characteristics of forging are indicated in Figure 88. Thick and thin sections can be drawn out of the metal at any part. Frequent and uniform annealing is essential to good forging practice.

Fig. 86.

Fig. 87.

Fig. 88.

CHAPTER 4

THE HAMMERS

During the metal craftsman's working life he will gather many tools. Some will be used almost daily, others infrequently, and some may be made especially for a specific purpose, to be used only once.

On this and succeeding pages is illustrated a group of hammers—basic tools that I have found to be useful. These are the hammers used in the raising sequences described elsewhere.

The universal name designations of the hammers, so far as I know, have never been conclusively determined by any authority. For purposes of simplicity I have listed first the most widely accepted name for the tool and, in some instances, the alternative to that designation. The scale of the hammer may be determined by comparing it to the hand shown with the tool. The hand is intended, in addition, to suggest a typical handle grip. This will vary with the individual, of course. The weight of the hammer, in some instances, is given as an additional aid.

Fig. 89. Dome-faced Hammer, embossing hammer. Weight—1 pound

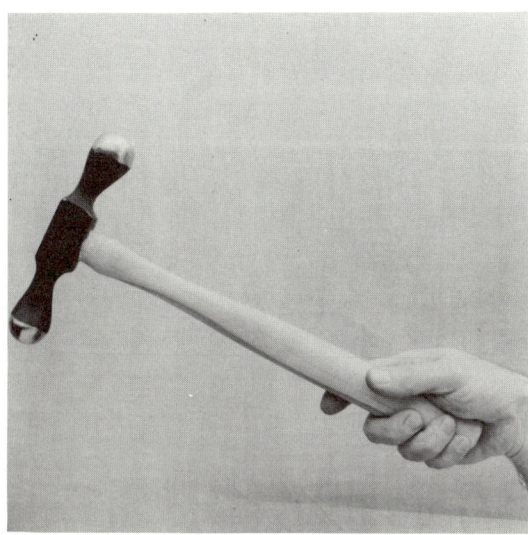

Fig. 90. Ball-faced Hammer, embossing hammer. Weight—1½ pounds

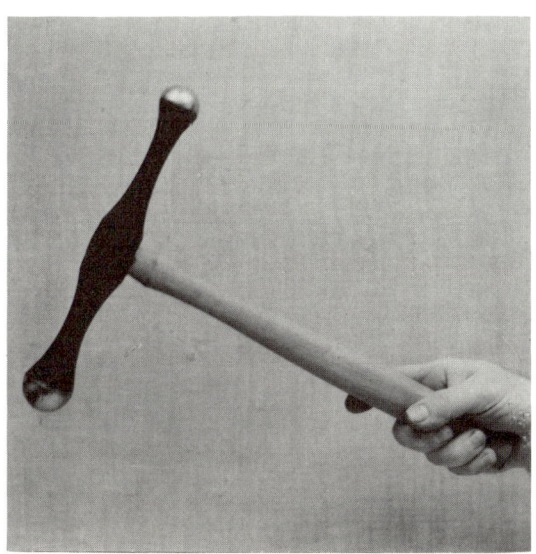

Fig. 91. Dome-faced Hammer, sinking hammer, embossing hammer. Weight—2½ pounds

Fig. 92. Ball-faced Hammer, bottoming hammer. Weight—1 pound

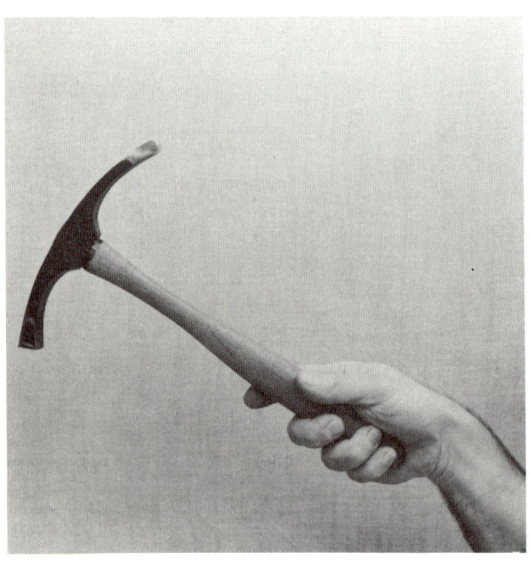

Fig. 93. Box Hammer. Weight—1 pound

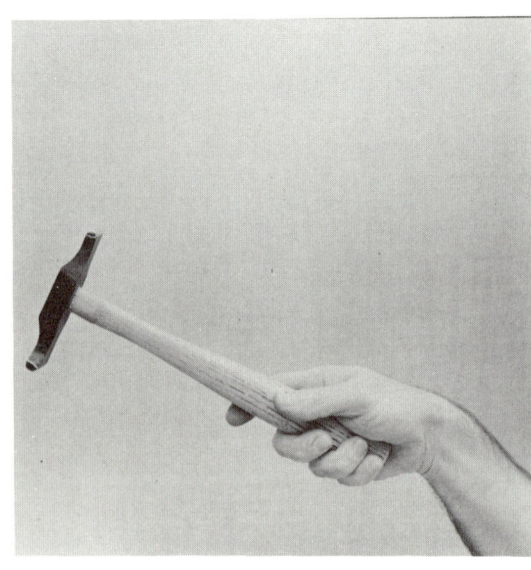

Fig. 95. Cross-peen Raising Hammer. Weight—12 ounces

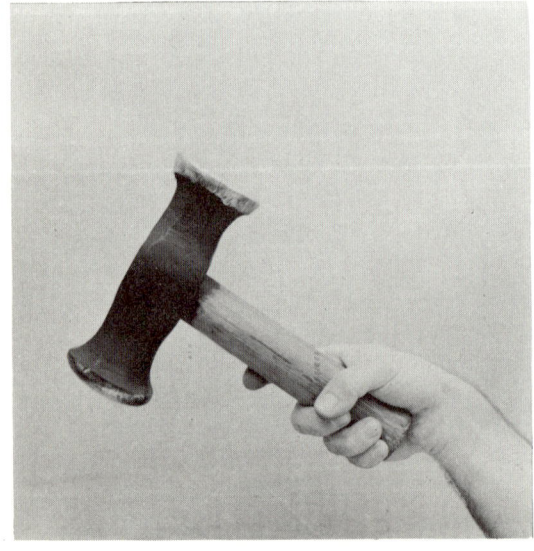

Fig. 94. Dome-faced Forging Hammer. Weight—6½ pounds

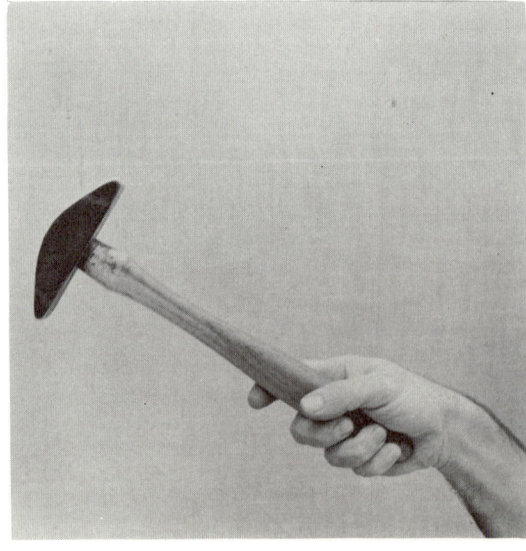

Fig. 96. Cross-peen Raising Hammer. Weight—1¼ pounds

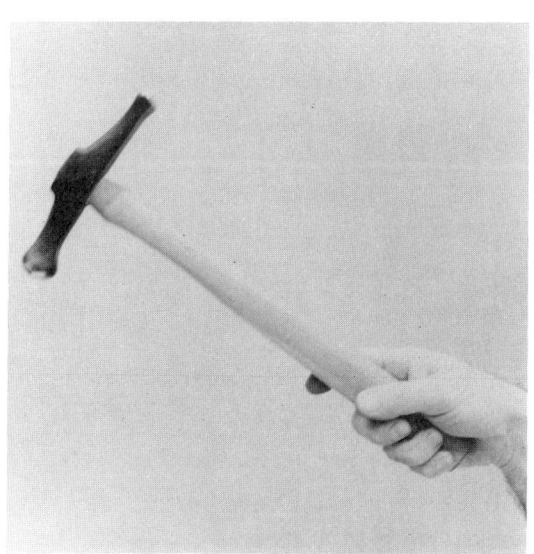

FIG. 97. Cross-peen Raising Hammer. Weight—1½ pounds

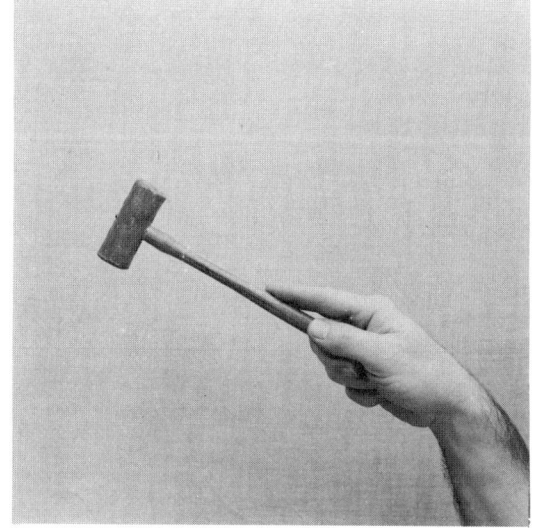

FIG. 99. Rawhide Mallet, small

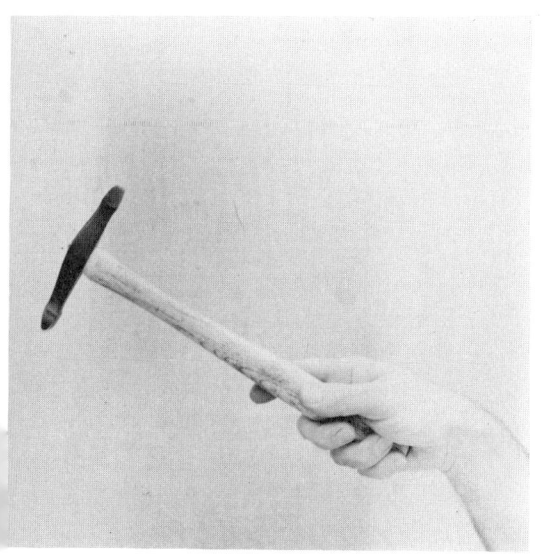

FIG. 98. Collet Hammer, neck hammer. Weight—9 ounces

FIG. 100. Rawhide Mallet, medium

Fig. 101. Rawhide Mallet, heavy. Weight—1¼ pounds

Fig. 102. Planishing Hammer, round-faced. Weight—½ pound

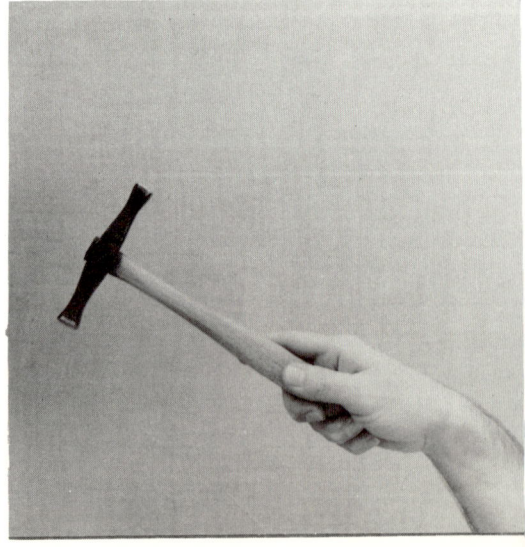

Fig. 103. Planishing Hammer, oval-faced. Weight—½ pound

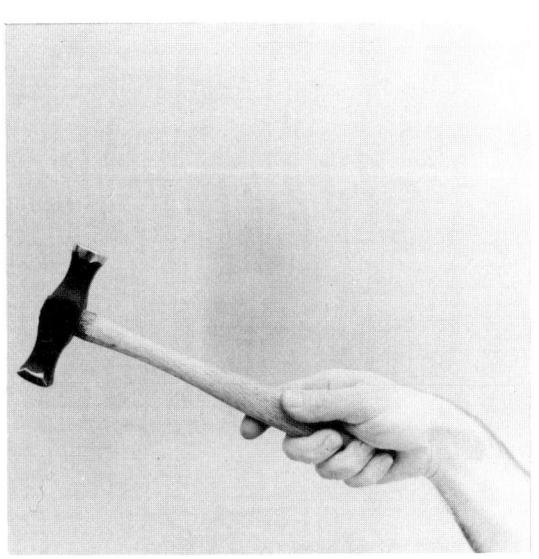

Fig. 104. Planishing Hammer, one round face, one square face. Weight—13 ounces

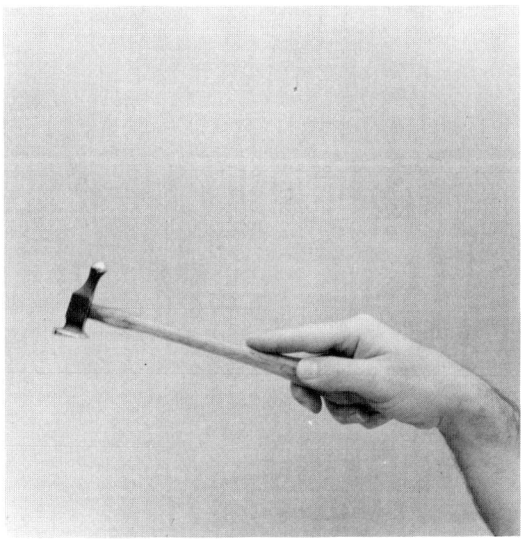

Fig. 106. Chasing Hammer. Weight—5 ounces

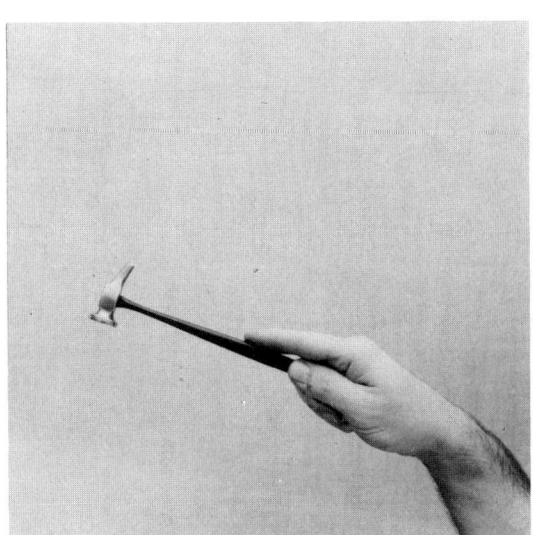

Fig. 105. Chasing Hammer, light. Weight—2 ounces

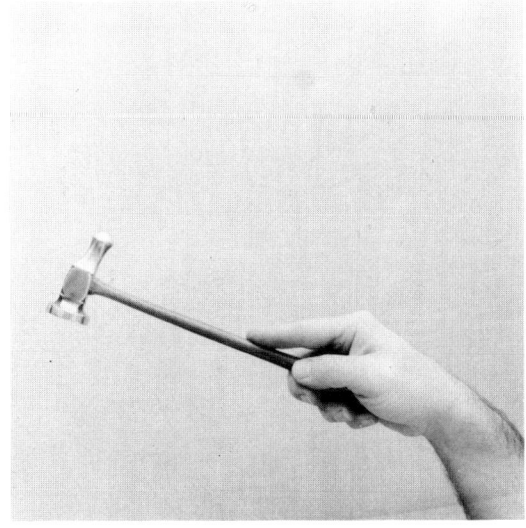

Fig. 107. Chasing Hammer, heavy. Weight—8 ounces

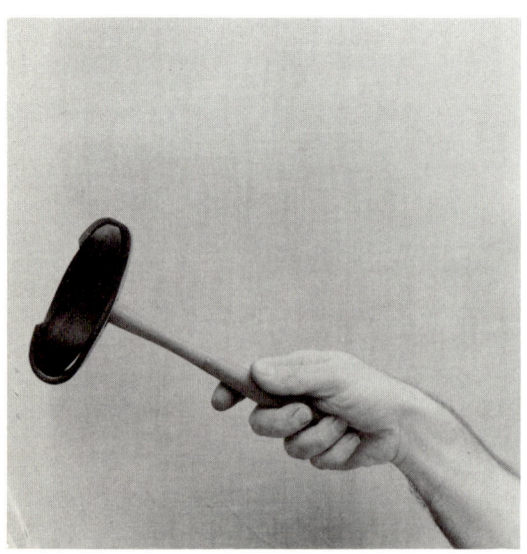

Fig. 108. Leather-faced Raising Mallet, wood

Fig. 109. Raising Mallet, wood

Fig. 110. Raising Mallet, wood, raising and box faces

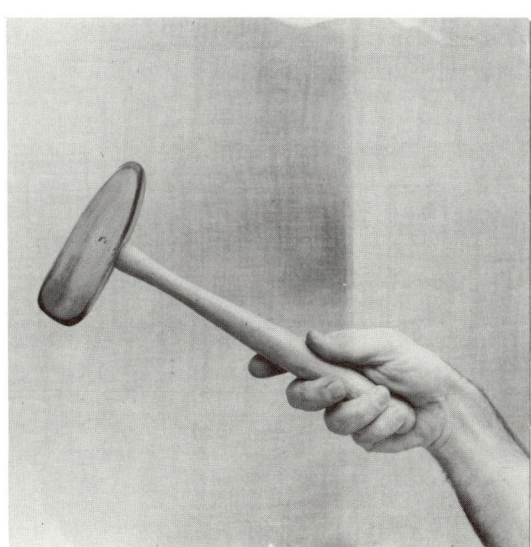

Fig. 111. Raising Mallet, wood, straight and cross-peen faces

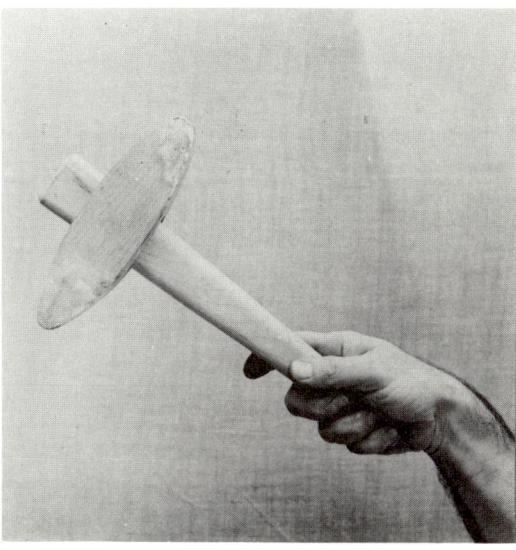

Fig. 113. Raising Mallet, wood. This hammer, with an inverted wedge handle and plastic reinforced working faces, is remarkably useful despite the clumsy appearance

Fig. 112. Horn Mallet, horn-tip mallet

Fig. 114. Mallet, wood. This hammer was especially turned from hard maple for sinking lead

CHAPTER 5

THE TOOL AND ITS USE

As with hammers, the metalsmith will provide himself with a sound collection of stakes, anvils, surface plates, and other devices against which his work is formed. To the armorer, and to his lineal descendents, the contemporary metalsmith owes much for the simple elegant forms—and the colorful names—of his stakes. The forms of the stakes have resulted from selection by trial and discard, until those that have survived to our times are models of function—they suggest a use. The names of these stakes, which have survived with them—Sparrow-hawk, Beakhorn, Candlemold, Blowhorn, Needlecase, Conductor, Bickiron, Horse and Crank, Snarling Iron, Cow's Tongue, Throw-back Iron—provide an interesting insight to the smith's high regard for his tools.

In the following illustrations are shown a group of stakes and accessories, combined with a possible use. The use is not the only one for which

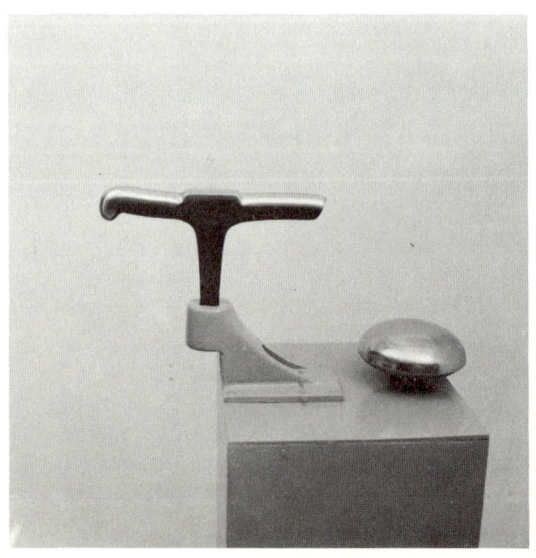

FIG. 115. Common T-stake. The stake is set in a cast stake holder, attached to a heavy block of wood called the "Steady"

the stake is designed. For other uses, refer to the section of this book concerned with raising processes.

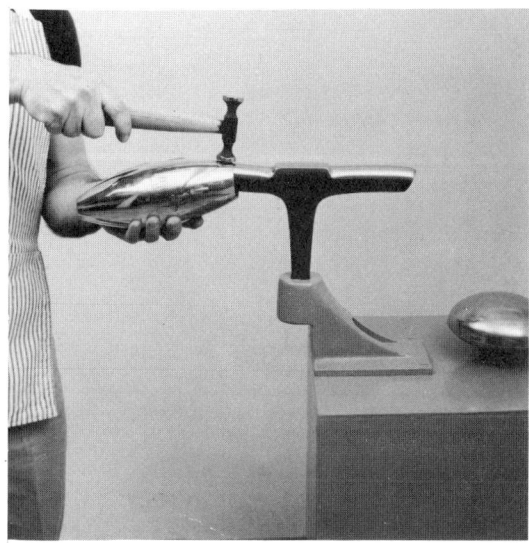

FIG. 116. Planishing a deep vessel on the common T-stake

FIG. 117. Common T-stake

FIG. 118. Planishing an open vessel on a common T-stake

Fig. 119. Common T-stake

Fig. 121. Common T-stake

Fig. 120. Planishing the rim on a "raised-in" vessel on the slight concave surface of a common T-stake

Fig. 122. Planishing the curve on a "raised-in" vessel on a common T-stake

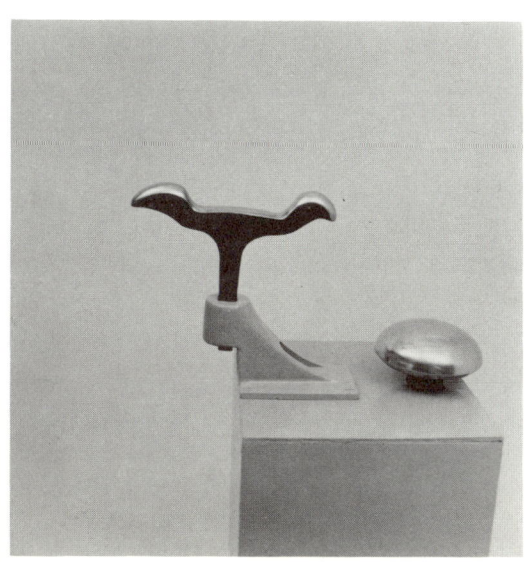

FIG. 123. Cow's Tongue Stake

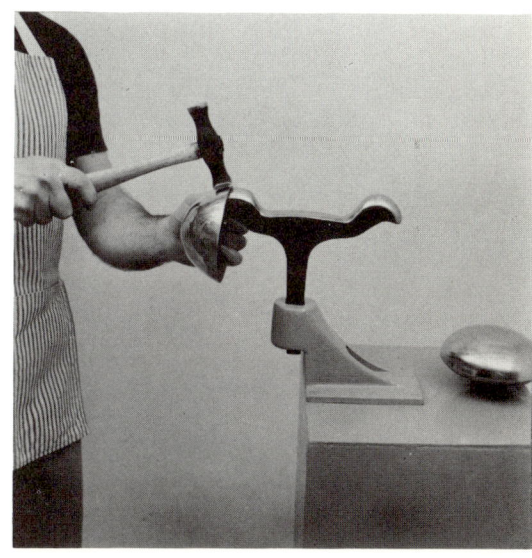

FIG. 124. Planishing the curve on an open vessel on the Cow's Tongue

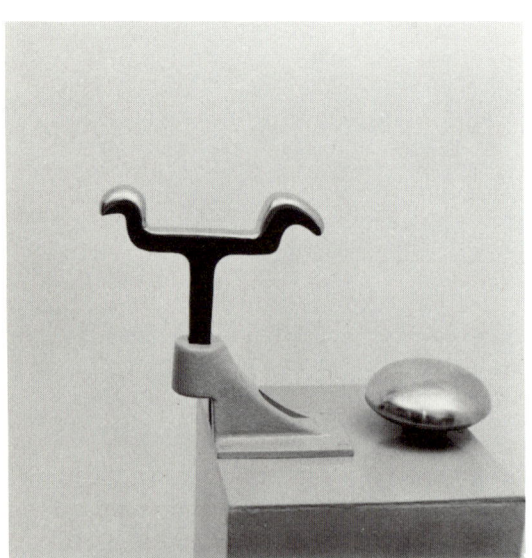

Fig. 125. Spout Stake

Fig. 127. Another version of the Spout Stake

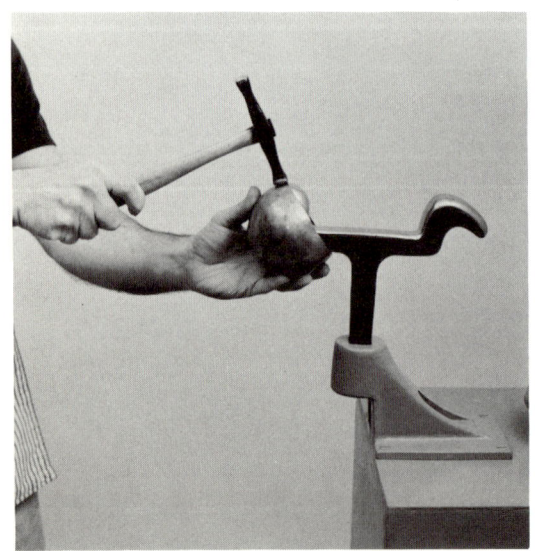

Fig. 126. Planishing the curve of a closed vessel on the Spout Stake

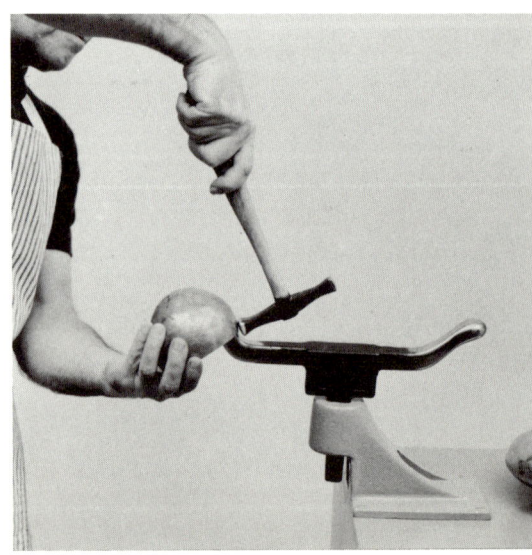

Fig. 128. Planishing the plane of a straight-sided open vessel on the Spout Stake

Fig. 129. Concave T-stake

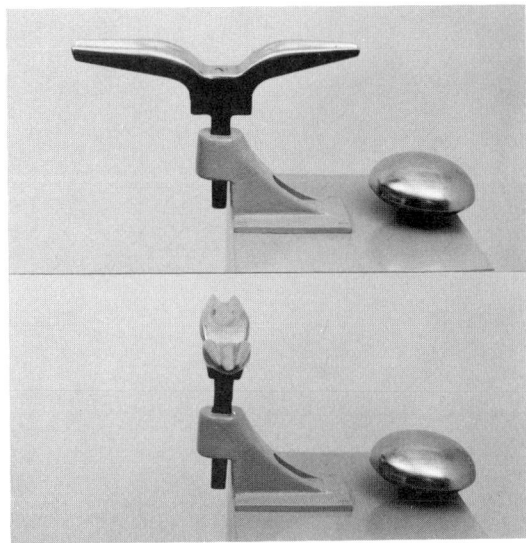

Fig. 131. Valley Stake, side and end views

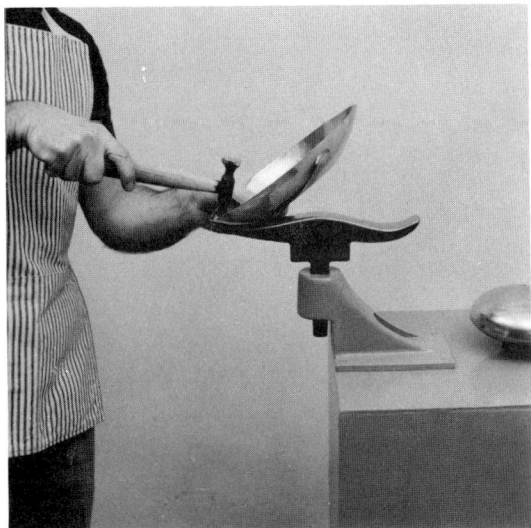

Fig. 130. Planishing the inside curve of an open vessel on the concave surface of the T-stake

Fig. 132. Sinking grooves on the Valley Stake in preparation for raising by the crimping method

Fig. 133. Heavy Side Stake, fitted in a square hole in the wood block "Steady"

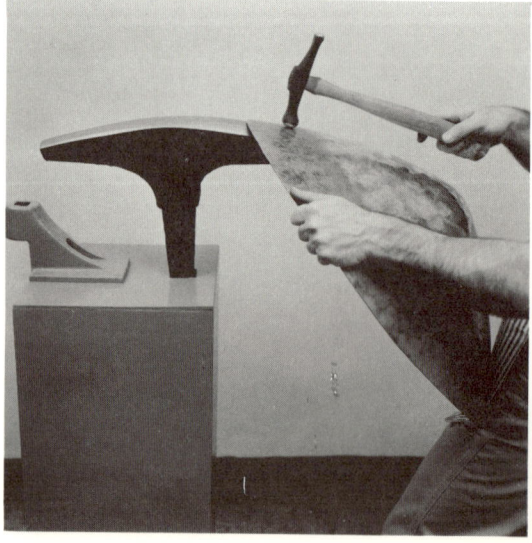

Fig. 134. Raising a large open vessel on the Side Stake

Fig. 135. Common T-stake, heavy

Fig. 137. Vertical Ball Stake

Fig. 136. Raising an angle on the T-stake

Fig. 138. Planishing an open vessel on the Ball Stake

Fig. 139. Vertical Dome Stake

Fig. 141. Heavier version of the Vertical Dome Stake

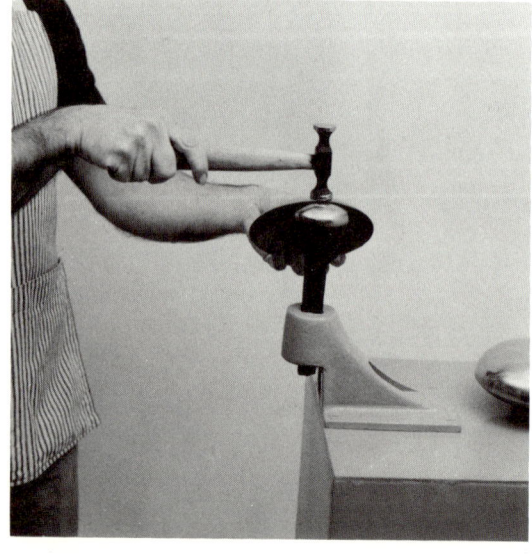

Fig. 140. Planishing an open vessel on the Dome Stake

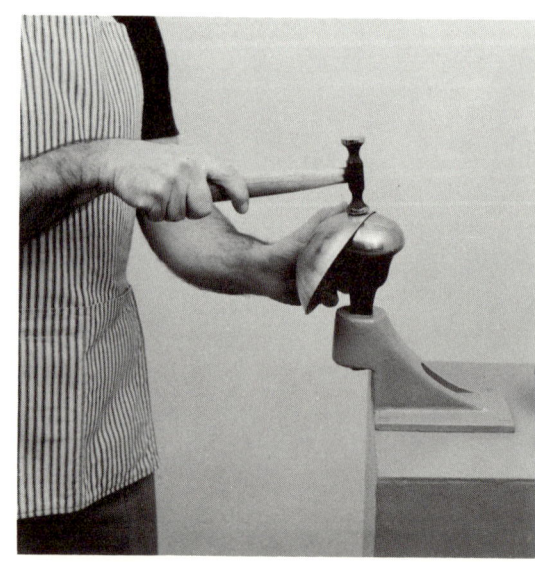

Fig. 142. Planishing on open vessel on the Dome Stake

Fig. 143. Vertical Half Dome Stake

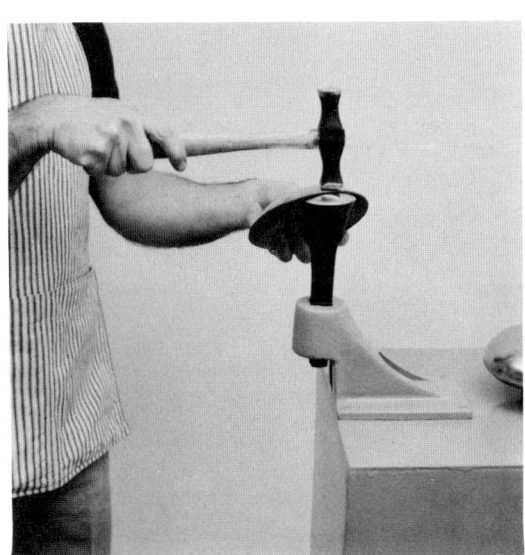

Fig. 144. Planishing a flat open vessel on the Half Dome Stake

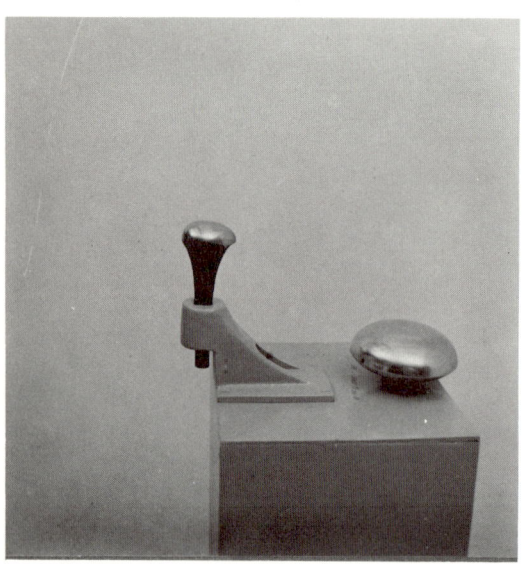

Fig. 145. Vertical Spoon Stake

Fig. 146. Planishing a spoon bowl on the Spoon Stake

Fig. 147. Vertical Bottoming Stake

Fig. 149. Vertical Bottoming Stake with an extender

Fig. 148. Squaring the flat bottom of an open vessel

Fig. 150. Squaring the flat bottom of a deep vessel

Fig. 151. Horse, fitted with a Head (left), an Extender, and a Coppersmith's Square Head (right)

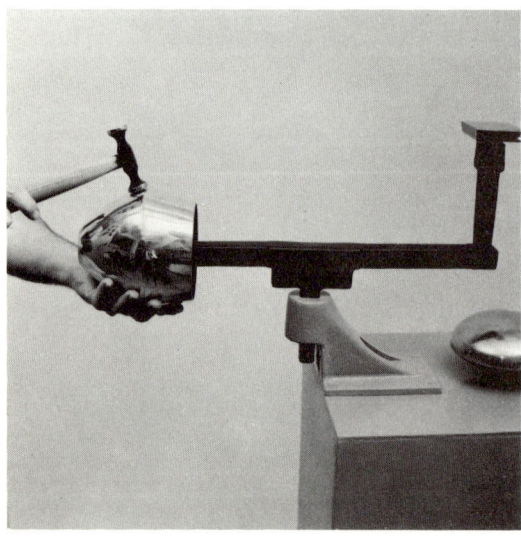

Fig. 152. Planishing an angle on a deep closed vessel.

Fig. 153. Another version of the Cow's Tongue Stake. This type must be held in a vise. The vise weighs 65 pounds and is secured to a heavy oak stump

Fig. 155. Version of a Spout Stake, vise-held

Fig. 154. Planishing a flared shape on the Cow's Tongue Stake

Fig. 156. Forging a concave spoon shank on the Spout Stake

Fig. 157. Crank Stake, vise-held

Fig. 159. Crank Stake, vise-held

Fig. 158. Planishing a small closed vessel on the Crank Stake

Fig. 160. Planishing a closed vessel on the Crank Stake

69

Fig. 161. Mandrel, vise-held

Fig. 162. Rounding out a ring on the Mandrel

Fig. 163. Snarling Iron, vise-held. This tool depends upon reflex action to perform its function. A steel bar held in the right hand delivers the blow at the point indicated

Fig. 164. Raising a deep vessel with a Snarling Iron. As the horizontal section of the Snarling Iron is struck, the ball end is depressed and then springs back to deliver a blow to the inside surface of the vessel

Fig. 165. Blowhorn Stake. The stake is inserted in the square hole—the Hardy Hole—in the face of a blacksmith's anvil

Fig. 166. Candlemold Stake, set in the Hardy Hole of the anvil

Fig. 167. Vertical Dome Stake, set in the Hardy Hole of the anvil

71

Fig. 169. Side Stake, wood, vise-held. This stake is made of hard maple.

Fig. 168. Vertical Bottoming Stake

Fig. 170. Raising an open vessel with a wood raising mallet on the Side Stake

Fig. 171. Valley Stake, wood, vise-held

Fig. 172. Sinking grooves on the Valley Stake with a wood raising mallet

SPINNING

Spinning is a mechanical means of raising. The process, although it requires skill and judgment, cannot be assumed to have the historic values of hand raising, and the object produced certainly should not be represented as a hand-wrought, handmade, or hand-fashioned piece. Spinning, however, does offer a particularly useful advantage to the individual craftsman if the need for a relatively large number of identical objects exists. Spun pieces too may be modified by hand raising after they have been removed from the lathe. This is a perfectly legitimate means and one that offers exciting design possibility. One, of course, would not describe a hand-modified spun piece as a hand-raised object.

The traditional differentials between the definitions of hand and machine techniques are held with great tenacity by various individuals and groups devoted to the practice and perpetration of the practices of earlier artisans. As opposed to this view, I would suggest that the great craftsmen of the past achieved a significant part of their greatness by being the innovators of their times. If we accept without question the recommendations of the past, which could not possibly predict with complete accuracy the technical, aesthetic, social, economic, and other conditions that we now enjoy, we are in default. The use of spinning as a normal complement to the skills of the metal craftsman is a particularly sensitive subject to the adherents of traditional attitude, but I believe the process to be of no less (and no greater!) importance than the process of hand raising.

CHAPTER 6

Almost any sturdy lathe may be used for spinning, but a variable-speed machine with heavy thrust bearings is desirable.

For the most part, the finished spun product is an open symmetrical shape. It is possible to spin closed shapes and asymmetrical shapes, but these techniques are complex, require special skills and knowledge, and are not essential for the small shopworker.

The Process

The chuck or pattern over which the metal is forced by the tool is made of wood or steel. The wood form is normally made of well-seasoned maple and is turned to shape on the lathe with the use of wood turning tools and tool rest. The wood block may be attached to the power head with a face plate that fits the threads of the power head, or the block may be drilled, tapped with threads conforming to the power head of the lathe, and attached directly.

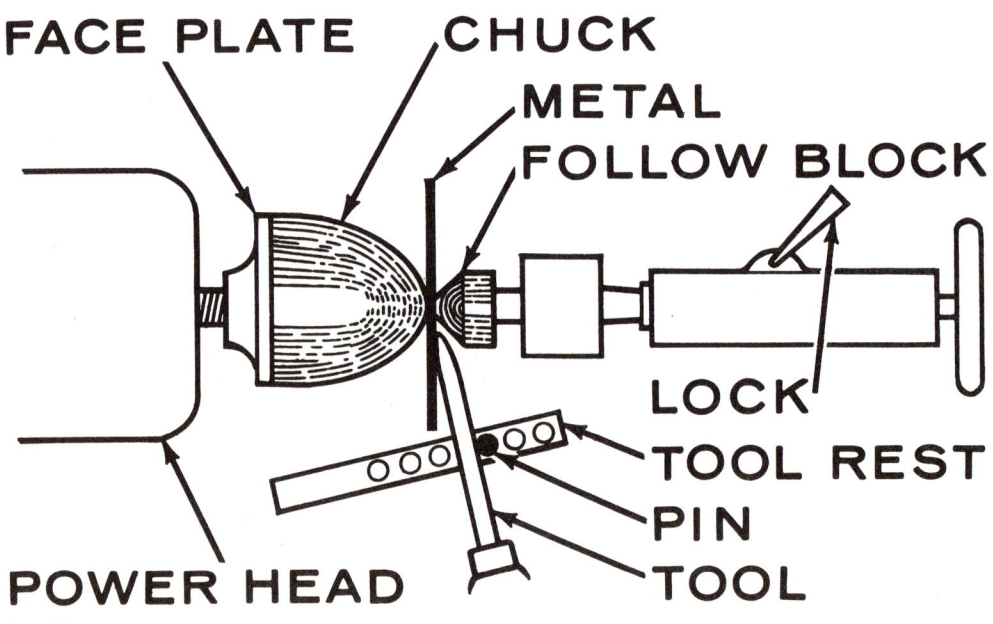

Fig. 173.

When the desired shape in wood is turned and sanded, the wood turning tool rest is removed and a spinning rest is substituted. The spinning rest is a horizontal bar with equally spaced holes drilled along the surface to receive a pin which acts as the fulcrum for the spinning tools. Figure 173 shows a plan view of a lathe setup for spinning.

The spinning tools are made of highly polished steel, fitted with wood handles. They may be three feet long and correspondingly heavy, but for normal use a shorter version is used. The shapes of the tools vary, but the most valuable ones are ball-shaped at the working end, flattened or spoon-shaped, and softly pointed. In addition, a hard wood wedge shape is useful.

In the following group of sequence photographs is a typical spinning operation.

In Figure 174, the chuck has been completed and the spinning tool rest with the fulcrum pin is in place. The

Fig. 174.

Fig. 175.

machine is ready to receive the metal disk. The disks for spinning are cut from any of the reasonably worked elemental or alloy metals. The thickness may vary, but of course very thin and very heavy sheets are not desirable. For the first few trials I would suggest uniformly annealed 16-gauge (.051) copper.

The metal disk is inserted at the face of the chuck and secured by running the follow block up against it firmly. Then, as illustrated in Figure 175, the disk is centered by wedging the wooden tool lightly between the fulcrum pin and the edge of the disk, which the machine is turning over slowly. This action must be co-ordinated with increased and decreased pressure exerted by the follow block by turning the tail stock wheel. When the piece is centered, run the follow block in firmly and lock the tail stock assembly. Note: In this and following operations the worker should wear protective goggles against possible injury from flying metal, lubricating compounds, et cetera.

Fig. 176.

Fig. 177.

When the lathe is at rest, pick up the lubricating tallow on the finger tip and apply it to the surface of the metal to be worked, as illustrated in Figure 176. Tallow mixed with oil is the most common lubricant, but soap or commercially prepared water-soluble compounds are also used.

In Figure 177, the work is begun by starting the lathe, inserting the tool (the pointed tool) to the left of the fulcrum pin, as close to follow block as possible and in contact with the metal. The butt of the tool should be placed high under the right arm against the side of the body. This offers additional mechanical advantage, because the entire weight of the upper body may be used to apply pressure to the tool. The tool face should ride over the metal in firm, constant pressure from the center to the outer rim. It is helpful to visualize the chuck form and make the tool conform to that shape, rather than to repeat the form of the metal.

In Figure 178, the work is progressing. The work conforms to the chuck near the center, but is free at the edge. It may be necessary at this point to remove the piece from the lathe and anneal it. Do not try to work the metal too far until you gain confidence and experience.

In Figure 179, the pointed tool has been exchanged for the spoon-shaped one to take advantage of the larger surface area in contact with the work. The work proceeds as before—from the center to the edge.

At this point (see Figure 180) the metal is fitted to the chuck and is being burnished down evenly. Before

Fig. 178.

Fig. 179.

you reach this stage, some difficulty may arise because of buckling or wrinkling of the edge. If this should happen (and it frequently does!) remove the piece, anneal, and remove the wrinkles by bumping them out with a rawhide mallet with the work held over a vertical stake. If the wrinkles become pleats and begin to fold under, quickly stop work, anneal the piece, and remove the pleats—or, better yet, discard the piece!

In Figure 181, the spinning is complete and the edge is being forced to the chuck. The tool rest and pin may be removed and the surface worked down with abrasive papers in preparation for buffing and polishing.

After the metal has been burnished to the chuck and cleaned, the edge may be dressed with the cutting tool. Replace the tool rest and pin and lay the cutting tool against the edge. The tool must be very sharp, and it is better to cut from the uneven edge back toward the center rather than attempt to cut through the metal. Keep your head

Fig. 180.

Fig. 181.

and as much of your hands and forearms as possible out of line with the cut. Of course, goggles should be worn, for as the metal is cut the chips will fly!

To remove the completed work, back off the tail stock and slip the piece off the chuck. If it does not slip off easily, check the cut edge to make certain a burr has not been pressed into the wood. If this has happened, recut the edge slightly at right angles to the main axis of the side of the form and make certain that the burr is removed. If the shape still clings to the chuck, set up the tool rest and fulcrum pin and, with the flat side of the spoon tool as a lever, try to wedge the piece off by applying pressure at the edge, while the lathe is turning over slowly. In this case the follow block should be backed off about $1/4''$ to hold the piece loosely in place when the wedging action forces it off. If the piece still will not budge from the form, it is likely that so much pressure was used in the final burnishing stage that the metal conforms to the minute irregularities of the wood surface so perfectly that removal is impossible. If you want to save the piece, remove the chuck and its metal sheath from the lathe and burn the wood out! Better yet, don't try to save the piece, but dump it in the nearest trash can, secure in the knowledge that it has happened to the best metal spinners and that you have learned a great deal about metal spinning!

Fig. 182.

CHAPTER 7

SAND CASTING

Sand casting is a method of reproducing in metal an object—usually an especially prepared wood model—with the use of bonded sand as the mold impression retainer.

Contemporary industrial sand-casting techniques are highly developed. I have seen instances where thumbprints, perhaps carelessly left by the pattern maker on the wax filleting material, have been reproduced faithfully in detail. While it is not likely that the industrial foundryman is particularly interested in reproducing a fingerprint, it does indicate the advances that have been made in the industry by reason of finer and more durable molding techniques and metal control. For the individual craftsman, sand casting as a process offers a useful and relatively inexpensive method for achieving massive quality in his work.

In Figures 183, 184, 185, 186, 187, 188, 189, and 190 are illustrated parts of a group of sixteen panels—the

Fig. 183.

Fig. 184.

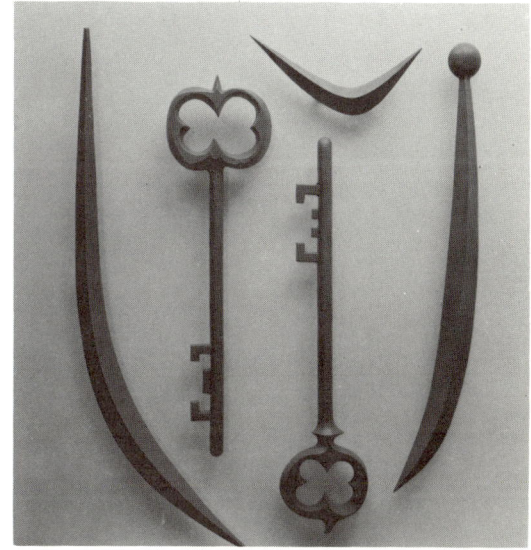

Fig. 186.

Fig. 185.

Fig. 187.

symbols of the Evangelists and the Apostles, designed by the author for the Concordia Senior College, Fort Wayne, Indiana. Except for the heads of the Man, the Lion, and the Eagle, which were prepared in plaster by Sculptor Jon Rush, the elements for the panels (30″ x 30″) were carved directly in mahogany by Ernest Toth and the author and were cast by foundrymen (DeGuilio Foundry, Ferndale, Michigan) whose primary work is industrial in nature. Casting followed normal procedures.

The Process

The following photographic sequence and the written text describes a small-scale simple sand-casting process.

Figure 191 illustrates initial sifting of a bit of sand on a steel surface plate as a protective layer for the intricately detailed silver medallion being reproduced. (Incidentally, potential forgers should not consider this means of reproducing coins! The cost

Fig. 188.

Fig. 189.

Fig. 190.

per unit in production and the cost of raw metals could exceed the value of the finished pieces!) The sand is sifted through a piece of ordinary screening.

In Figure 192, the medallion is centered on the sand and lightly pressed into place.

A cast-iron box with an interior concave section is placed over the medallion. (This half of the box is called the "cope." The other half of the box is called the "drag," and the two halves assembled are called a "flask.") Again, some sand is lightly sifted over the surface of the medallion to assure a fine uniform coating which will receive and hold the impression. (See Figure 193.)

The cope is filled with sand, mounded up and pressed into the concave depressions inside the box. You will note that, when compressed, the sand will hold its shape. There are two main reasons why the sand holds its shape—the structure of the particles of sand and a tempering or bonding agent that is mixed with it. The sand may be

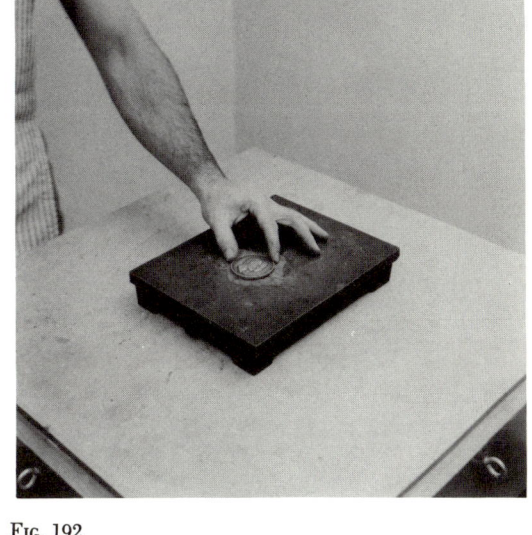

FIG. 192.

FIG. 191.

FIG. 193.

mixed with oil (glycerine), but for the best results only water is used because the water can be driven off before casting. This eliminates the formation of steam, which can "blow back" and cause porous, incomplete casting. (See Figure 194.)

In Figure 195, the sand is rammed down over the model with a wooden mallet. Many light blows with the mallet are better for this purpose than a few heavy ones. Make certain that the entire cope is uniformly filled and that pressure is equally distributed throughout the mass.

With a steel straightedge level the surface of the sand in the cope, as illustrated in Figure 196.

Turn the cope over, being careful not to dislodge the model. Carefully loosen the sand adhering to the face of the model and brush it away with a soft brush, as indicated in Figure 197.

With a knife blade or fine spatula cut a V-shaped groove from the embedded model to the sprue hole at the end of the flask. (I find a scalpel or

Fig. 194.

Fig. 195.

palette knife to be useful for this purpose.) If your flask does not have a sprue hole provided, you must cut the sprues through to the outside surface of the mold after the model has been extracted. Then cut carefully around the model to half its depth and at an angle of about 45°. Dust or blow out loose particles of sand (Figure 198.)

In order that the sand in the second half of the mold does not adhere to the sand in the cope, a thin layer of talc is dusted over the surface, as illustrated in Figure 199.

Leaving the cope half of the flask in position, place the drag half of the flask over it. The drag is equipped with pins that fit into drilled flanges on the cope. The holes in the flanges and the pins are usually placed off center so that misalignment of the two parts is practically impossible. Sift or riddle fine sand over the face of the exposed model, as shown in Figure 200.

In the drag, mound up the sand as before and press into place, as illustrated in Figure 201.

Fig. 197.

Fig. 196.

Fig. 198.

Fig. 199.

Fig. 200.

Fig. 201.

Fig. 202.

In Figure 202, the sand is again rammed into the concave sides of the flask and driven to the face of the model.

As before, square the surface of the sand by scraping with a steel straightedge. (See Figure 203.)

In Figure 204, the drag has been removed and laid aside. The cope is turned with the model face down. A few sharp raps on the side of the box will cause the model to drop free. If the model were made of wood and too light to drop of its own weight, pins could be inserted into it and the model drawn out.

In Figure 205, the drag half of the flask is now cleared of the positive half of the sprue hole which was reproduced by fitting into the cut channel in the cope half. This is done with a knife, as before. If you like, a second depressed channel or sprue may be cut into this volume of sand to assure a heavier column of metal in the sprue.

Figure 206 shows the two halves of the flask ready for reassembly. Note

FIG. 203.

FIG. 204.

that the sprue channel reaches the edge of the medallion impression.

Figure 207 illustrates an assembled flask and the pour. The flask faces, in this case, are backed up by plywood plates to support the sand. They are held in place by clamps. The metal is being poured in a continuous stream. (Once you start, don't stop until the cavity is filled.) Gloves and goggles are obviously necessary for protection against heat and possible "blow back."

After the metal has cooled, break open the mold, as illustrated in Figure 208.

The final photograph shows the finished casting with the sprue cut off. The casting in the left hand is the reproduction ready for filing and coloring. You will notice that the sand in the flask still retains the impression. Resist the temptation to try casting just once more into a used mold! (See Figure 209.)

Fig. 205.

Fig. 206.

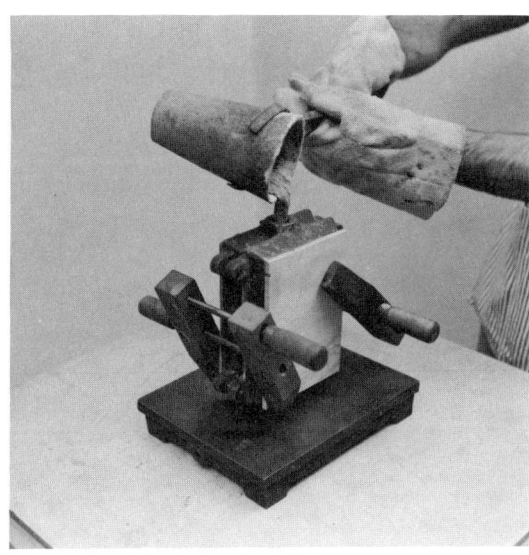

Fig. 207.

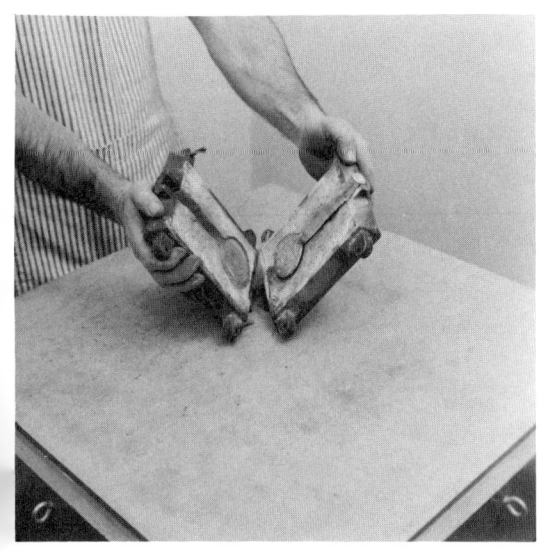

Fig. 208.

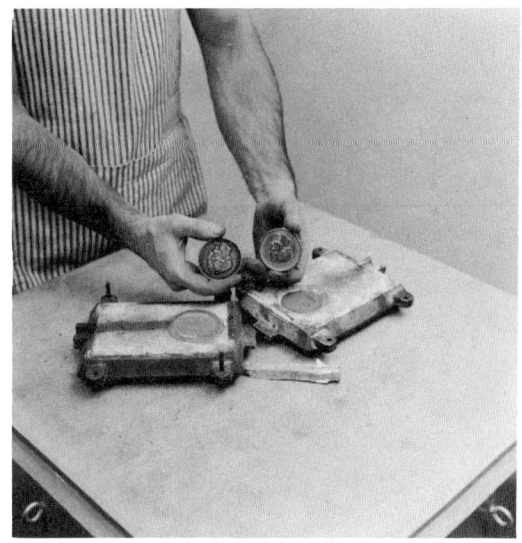

Fig. 209.

CHAPTER 8

INGOT MOLD

The working craftsman frequently finds himself with a surplus of scrap pieces of precious metal which, for one reason or another, cannot be used. These metal scraps may be returned to a workable state by casting them into a small ingot mold. The mold, of cast iron, is made with a fixed half and a sliding half so that the width of the finished ingot can be adjusted readily. The thickness of the mold cannot, unfortunately, be adjusted and in most commercially available models measures $\frac{1}{4}''$. The collected scrap can be melted in a crucible in an electric furnace, or an efficient muffle furnace can be made by erecting fire bricks in the annealing pan, placing the crucible within the contained space, and directing the air-gas flame of an annealing torch in a swirling manner through a hole at the base of the temporary muffle. Production air-gas furnaces of limited capacity are available at relatively low cost.

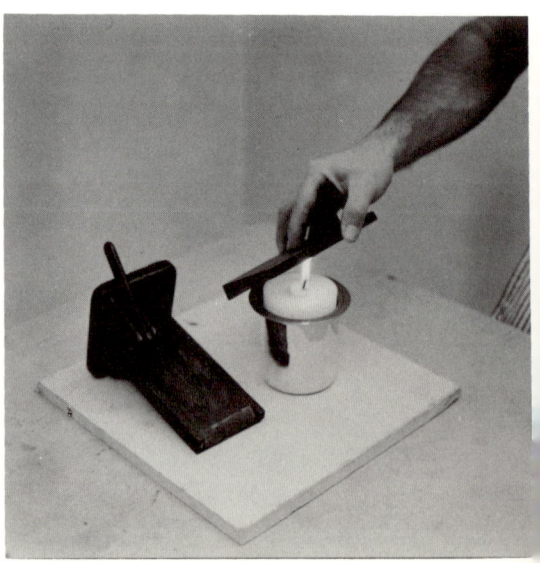

Fig. 210.

Ingot Mold—Casting

In Figure 210, the disassembled mold is being prepared by holding the interior surfaces over a candle flame to build up a uniform coat of carbon. This may also be done by coating the surfaces lightly with machine oil and then burning it off.

The scrap metal (only sterling silver, fine silver, or gold are worth recovering and are within the melting range of most small-shop equipment) is placed in a crucible and subjected to heat. A flux (borax) is added to combine with the oxides and keep the metal clean. As the metal melts, it should be stirred frequently with a steel rod. The rod should be allowed to heat well before it is introduced into the metal, or part of the molten mass will "freeze" to it. In Figure 211, the casting process is shown. The mold has been assembled and the attached clamp secured. The mold should be heated quite hot by playing a torch over it or by placing it in a furnace for a few minutes. The molten metal should be poured into the mold in one steady stream until the mold is full. Allow the metal to set for a few minutes; then break open the mold. The ingot will drop free, as illustrated in Figure 212.

Fig. 211.

Fig. 212.

CHAPTER 9

CENTRIFUGAL CASTING

Of all the means of casting available to the craftsman—injection casting, gravity casting (sand casting, described elsewhere in this book, is a form of gravity casting), air-pressure casting, vacuum casting, and centrifugal casting—the last-named has a unique value for its mechanical simplicity and fidelity of reproduction.

To dentistry—or, rather, to the technical and mechanical part of the field of dentistry—belongs the proper credit for the development of centrifugal casting, for it was the dental technician who refined the process at the demand of the practicing dentist (and his patients!) to replace the previous custom of peening malleable metal into cavities.

The Process

In the following photographic sequence and written descriptions I have reduced the process to its simplest terms, in the hope that the individual small-shop craftsman will elaborate and adjust according to his need.

In Figure 213, the model, a reproduction in wax of a coin, is shown with preformed wax wire, the wax tool, the sprue former, and a Bunsen burner for heating the tool. The burner is mounted on a block to hold it at an angle so that wax will not foul the tube if it should drop off the tool.

In Figure 214, the wax wires are attached to the base of the model by passing the blade of the hot tool between the end of the wire and the model. (A description of sprue systems follows this sequence. Refer to it now.)

The wax wires with the model attached are gathered, slightly warmed over the burner, and twirled between the thumb and forefinger to round them into a single mass. This single wire is then "welded" to a small ball of wax at the small end of the funnel-shaped sprue former. (See Figure 215.)

The model and wax wires (sprues) are now carefully painted with a wetting agent (debubblizer). (See Figure 216.) This permits the water and plaster mix to flow evenly over the wax which, if it were not so treated, would not "fit" the model, because the water in the plaster would be repelled by the wax surface.

In Figure 217, a creamy mixture of plaster and water is shown being carefully applied to the surface of the model. The wax wires should also be covered with this mixture. The plaster should not be painted directly on the wax, but rather should be dropped in small blobs, which are then settled into place by vibrating the whole assembly

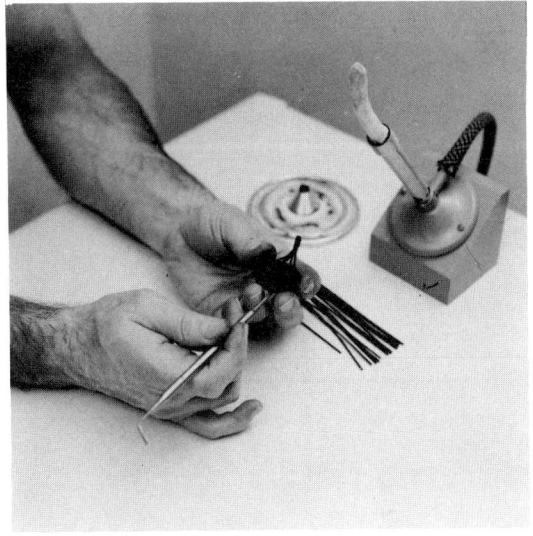

Fig. 214.

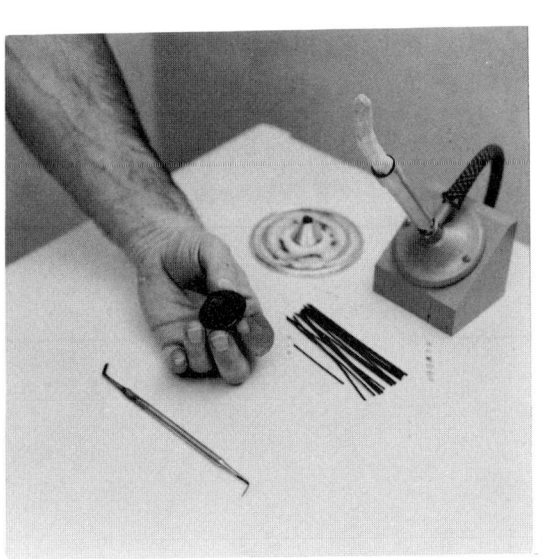

Fig. 213.

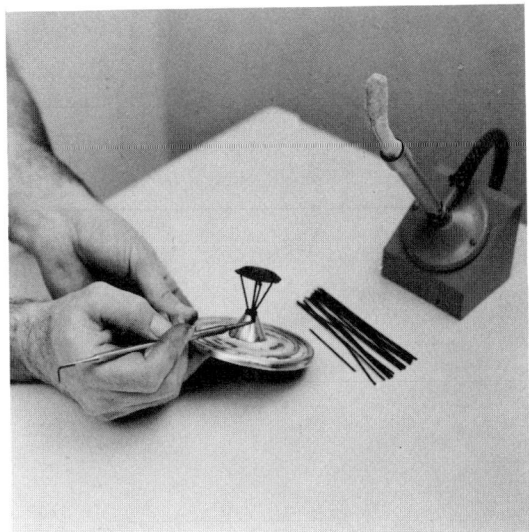

Fig. 215.

by gently tapping the sprue former. The plaster is a special type, highly resistant to the stresses of temperature change. "Cristobalite," made by the Kerr Manufacturing Company, Detroit, Michigan, is excellent for this purpose.

In Figure 218, a steel cylinder (flask or ring) is prepared by lining it with sheet asbestos. This may be done easily by wrapping a length of the strip around the outside of the cylinder, tearing it off to size, and then inserting it inside. After the whole inside surface has been covered with the strips in this manner, the flask is immersed in water and the asbestos modeled to the interior shape with the fingers. The lining permits the plaster to "move" under the stresses of heat.

The lined flask is placed on a smooth surface (see Figure 219) and a second mixture of plaster is poured into it to capacity. While the plaster is being poured, the side of the flask is tapped to facilitate the escape of entrapped air.

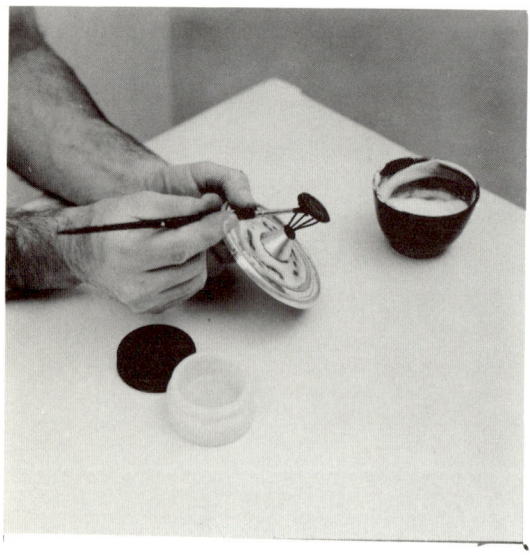

Fig. 216.

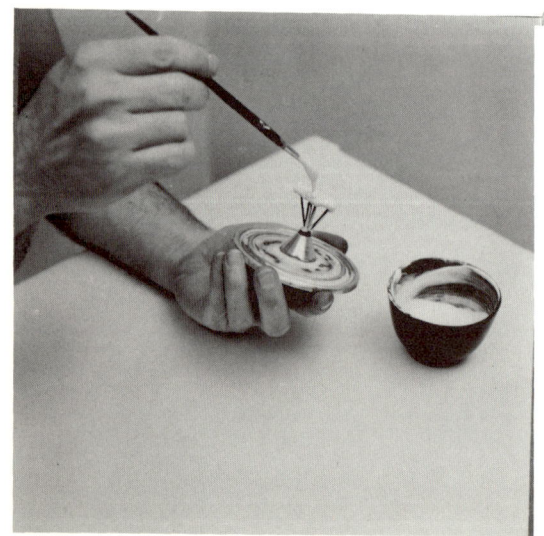

Fig. 217.

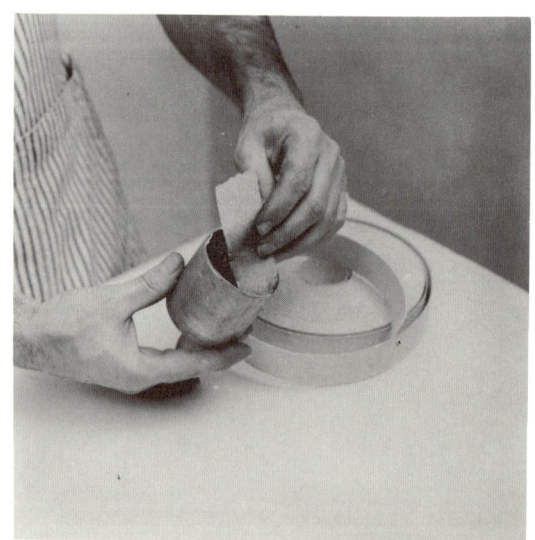

Fig. 218.

The invested model attached to the sprue former is inserted into the previously filled flask. (See Figure 220.) It is well to jiggle the hand during this process to help release air bubbles in the plaster.

After the sprue former and model with its attached wires are in place, the outer surface of the flask may be tapped again to assure final settling. (See Figure 221.) Be sure that the disk of the sprue former is centered on the flask. This will assure proper alignment with the crucible in the casting operation to follow.

After the plaster has set, knock off the sprue former. (See Figure 222.) This will leave a funnel-shaped depression in the plaster at the bottom of which you will see the gathered wax wires. The setting time of the plaster will vary. As a matter of convenience I usually allow the invested model to rest overnight.

Clean off the excess plaster on the outside of the flask. (See Figure 223.) This is important because, if the plas-

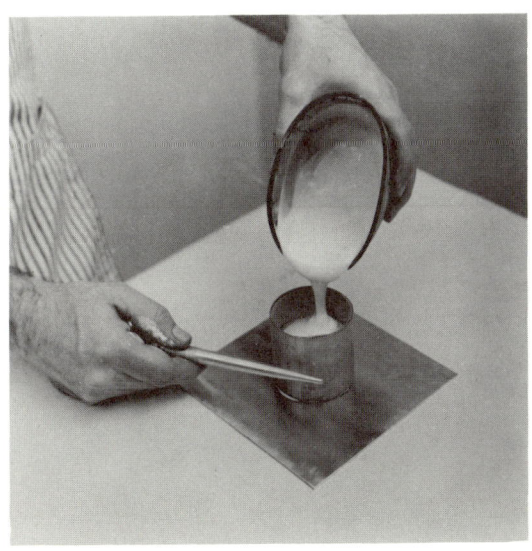

Fig. 219.

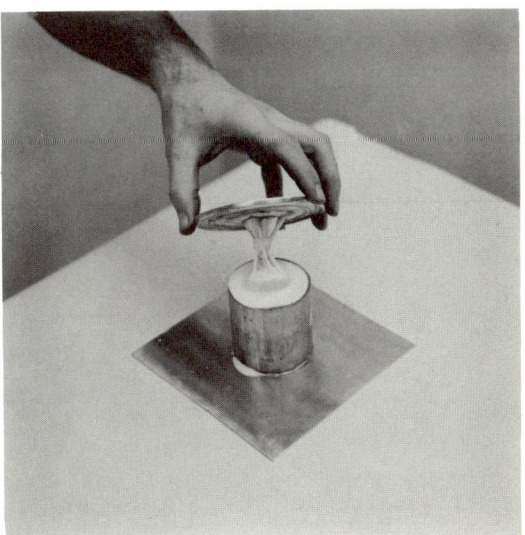

Fig. 220.

ter is allowed to remain, it will not permit the flask to seat properly in the carriage of the casting machine.

With tongs insert the flask into a preheated burn-out furnace, as illustrated in Figure 224. The heat should not exceed 800°F., but the interior temperature of the furnace is not especially important, provided, of course, it does not become too hot! Burn-out controls are desirable but not essential because the proper temperature and time can be determined by visual observation.

As the burn-out reaches its final stages, prepare the casting machine by selecting the proper carriage for the flask size you are using, by adjusting the counterbalancing arm to its proper place and by winding the machine against the resistance of the spring drive and locking it by bringing up the slide lock in the base of the machine. The number of turns—two or three—will be determined by experience. The completed burn-out can be determined by removing the flask from the fur-

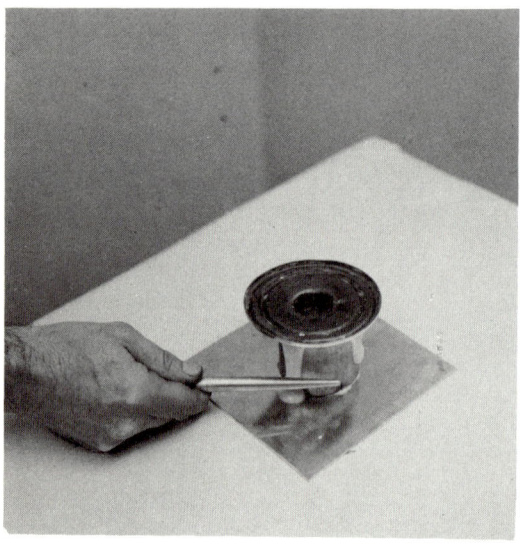

Fig. 221.

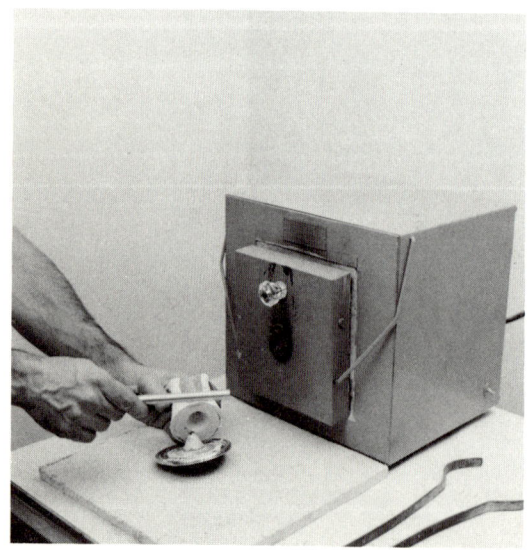

Fig. 222.

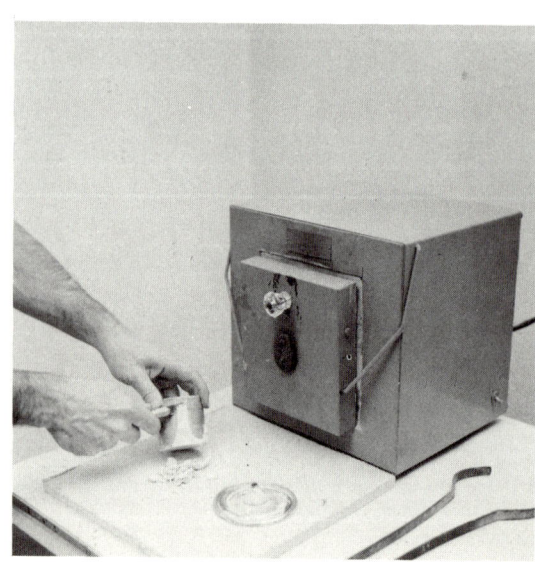

Fig. 223.

nace and observing the sprue hole. If the plaster has been restored to a white surface (the wax, as it burns, will leave a black deposit around the funnel-shaped hole) and the sprue holes at the base of the funnel are faintly pink, the burn-out is complete. Insert the flask in the casting machine with the tongs, as illustrated in Figure 225.

Put the metal to be cast into the crucible and melt it with a torch flame. (See Figure 226.) The amount of metal to be used for the specific casting can be determined by several means, but I find it much simpler to load the crucible to capacity. In this way one is certain of having enough metal and if too much is present, it will spill over, be caught by the protective shield, and can be used again.

When the metal is melted, pull the counterbalancing arm to you slightly. This will release the locking mechanism. Now raise both hands straight up at the same time. This will clear the torch hand and the holding hand from the path of the arm of the machine as

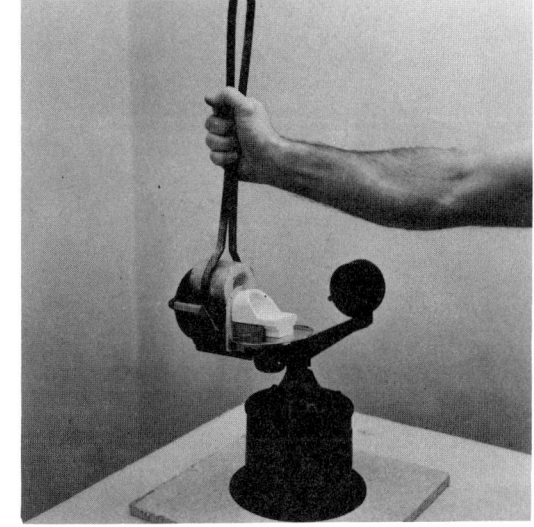

Fig. 225.

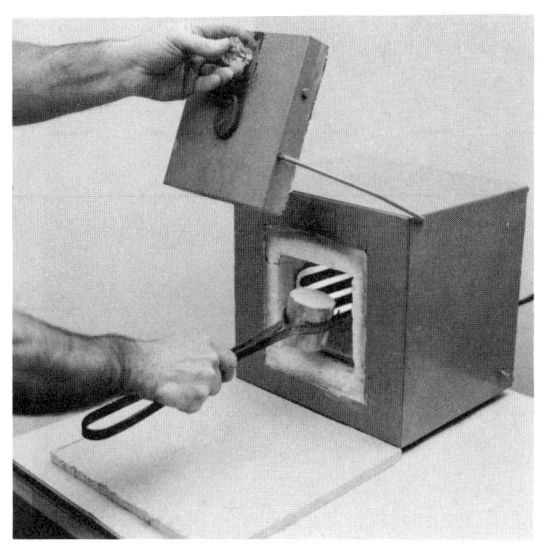

Fig. 224.

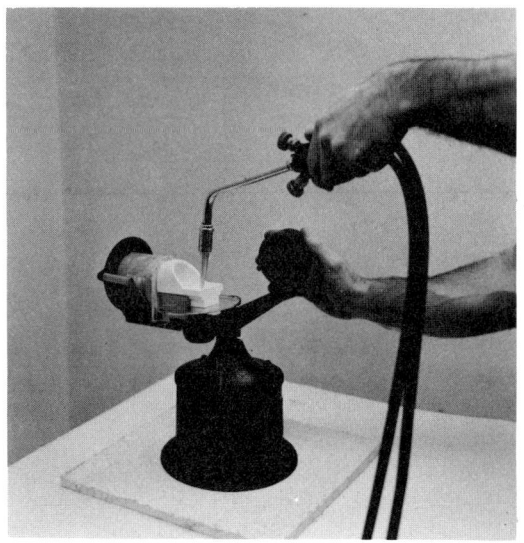

Fig. 226.

it swings. (See Figure 227. For the sake of simplicity in photographing this sequence, the protective shield that is normally placed around the casting machine has been eliminated.)

When the casting arm stops of its own accord, the metal has cooled, and the flask may be removed from its carriage with the tongs. Plunge the flask into a container of water. (See Figure 228.) The investment will disintegrate and the casting will drop free.

Clip the sprue wire from the casting. (See Figure 229.) The conical "button" indicates the excess metal that was trapped in the funnel-shaped hole in the plaster. This "button" is useful because its presence provides additional pressure in the casting process and thus makes possible a dense metal structure.

Figure 230 illustrates the accuracy of the centrifugal-casting method. The coin in the left hand is the reproduction just as it comes from the flask. It can now be finished and colored to match the original.

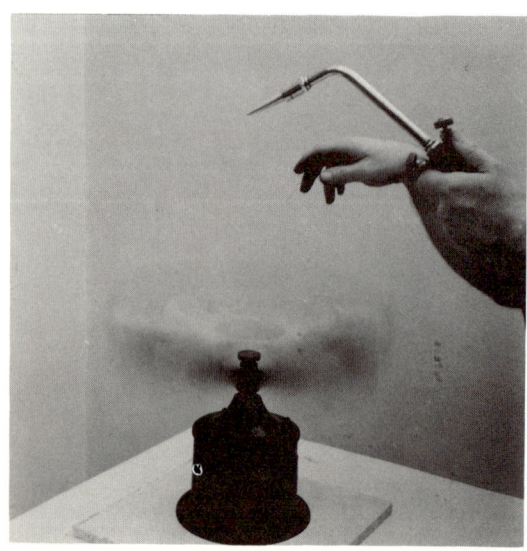

Fig. 227.

Fig. 228.

Intentionally I have not discussed the preparation of the wax model. Whether the original be carved from a block, modeled from a pliable wax, or cast in a metal or rubber mold, the choice is that of the individual craftsman.

In Figures 231 and 232 are illustrated four typical sprue systems that I have found to be useful.

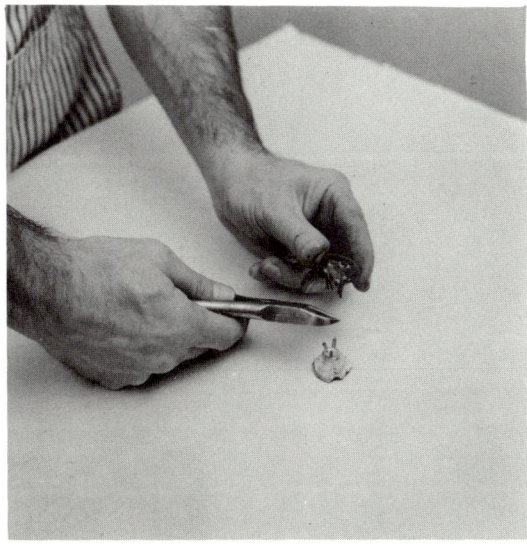

Fig. 229.

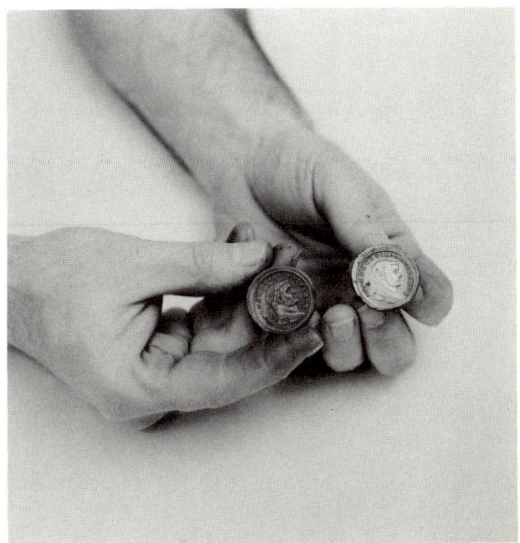

Fig. 230.

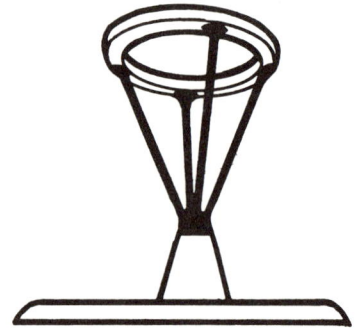

Fig. 231.

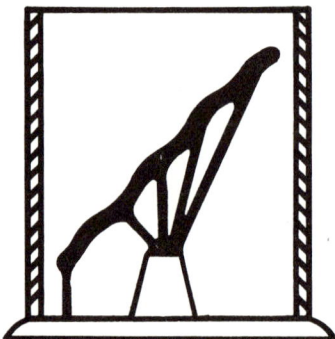

Fig. 232.

JOINING OF METALS

MONSTRANCE
By Florence Johnson Moursund
Cast Bronze, Raised Base, Gold Plate, 22″
(Photograph by Harvey Croze)

JOINING

Definition

The first man to work with metals must have become intrigued eventually with the possibility of joining one piece of fabricated or cast metal with another. When he finally learned to refine iron to make steel, he found an almost perfect way to join these metals by forge welding. Because of the highly sophisticated means available to us now—oxygen-acetylene torches, arc-welding devices, spot-welding machines, air-gas torches, and so on, for heating and fusing metals—forge welding belongs somewhere in the past with charcoal and bellows, but I cannot discuss joining of metals without a brief (and perhaps nostalgic) note about this method.

Forge welding of iron and steel and some other elemental metals depends upon heating the parts to be joined to a temperature just short of the flow point in an oxide free state and then subjecting the two parts to decisive blows with a hammer. Because the surface upon which the parts are laid for hammering, the hammer face, and the tongs holding the pieces will conduct heat away quite quickly, the smith has time for only one or two blows before the interior temperature drops below fusing range. In some instances one blow will weld and the second blow will "unweld"; so every hammer blow must count. The beautifully wrought Japanese Samurai swords were frequently built up by forge welding many layers of steel into one mass. The forge lines may be seen on the flat surfaces of old blades that have

CHAPTER 10

been etched by time and the elements. Figures 233 and 234 illustrate two means of preparing the stock for forge welding.

Soldering

Soldering is the most versatile and the simplest means of joining two pieces of metal. In general terms, the soldering process consists of flowing, in the presence of heat, a metal or alloy of metals between two separate like or unlike pieces of metal. Under proper conditions the flowing alloy may fuse with the surfaces of metals to be joined or will, by reason of molecular attraction, "fit" the two pieces so perfectly that a permanent bond is established.

Solders fall into two categories—hard and soft. I prefer to use the term "common solder" for all the soft solders, because it appears to be less confusing in discussion than "soft."

Perhaps the best way to differentiate between the two solder categories is to fix in mind firmly the critical temperatures and elemental composition of each.

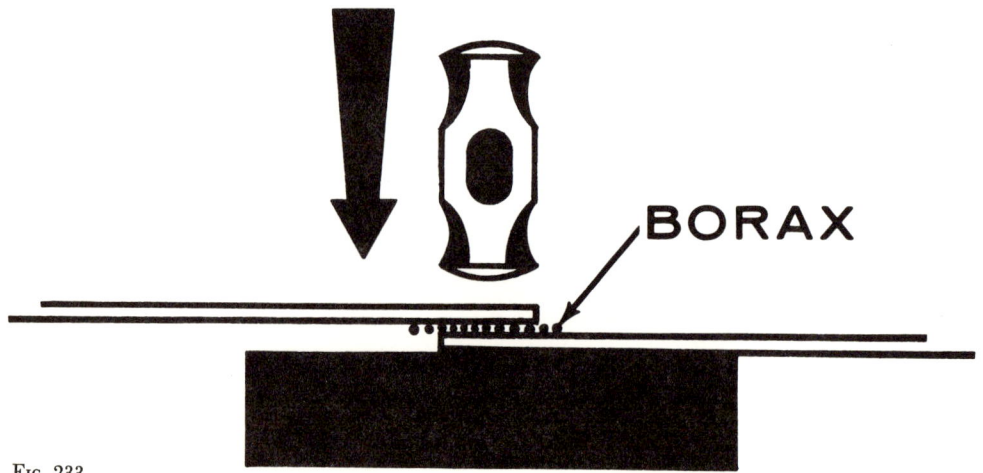

Fig. 233.

Common (or soft) solder is composed of lead and tin in various proportions—50 parts lead/50 parts tin, which melts at 450°F., or 60 parts tin/40 parts lead, which melts at 390°F. The alloy may be compounded in other proportions, but 50/50 and 60/40 are most useful. It is of interest that the alloys of common solders have a lower melting point than either of the components—tin, which melts at 465°F., and lead, which melts at 621°F. This is known as a "eutectic" alloy.

Hard solder is also a eutectic alloy in that its melting point, in alloy or "mixture," is lower than the lowest melting point of any of its major components.

Hard solder is a bit more complex in description. The most important hard solder is an alloy containing more than 50% silver and has a melting point ranging from 1450°F. to 1750°F. Hard solders containing less than 50% silver are called "silver brazing alloys" and have a flow point from 1070°F. to 1300°F.

For the purpose of simplicity, the

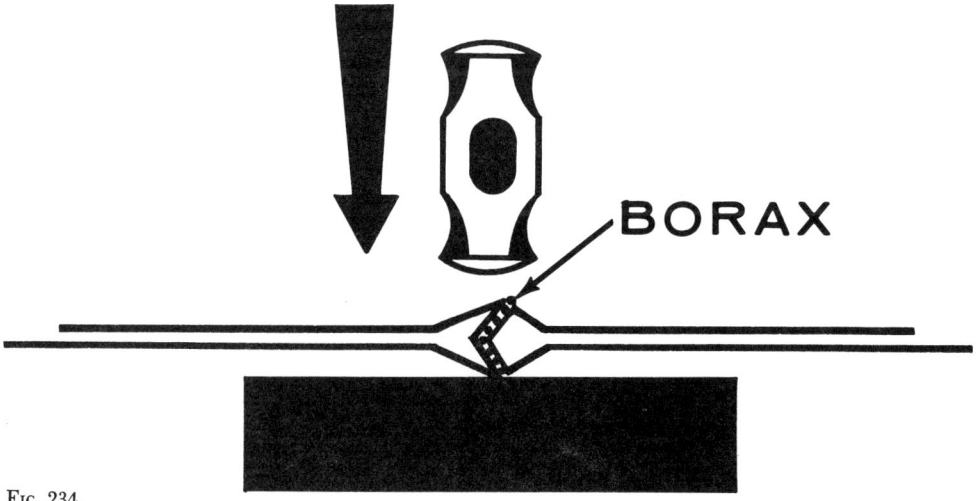

Fig. 234.

two alloys—those containing more than 50% silver and those containing less than 50% silver—will, from this point on, be considered "hard solder" or silver solder. The compositions of the hard solders vary considerably, as do their flow points and intended use.

For convenience the hard solders are further classified as "hard," "medium," and "easy," depending upon the critical temperature at which they melt. Hard has the highest flow point —approximately 1425°F.; medium flows at approximately 1390°F.; and easy melts at approximately 1325°F. Additional temperature ranges above and below these have been compounded and are called "extra hard," "extra easy," et cetera.

Note: Gold solders work very much like the hard or silver solders, have much the same temperature ranges, and are also classified as hard, medium, or easy. It is necessary, however, when one orders gold solders to specify color as well as melting-point characteristics.

In summary, the essential differences between common (or soft) solders and hard (or silver) solders lie in the elemental metals of which the alloys are composed and in the temperature ranges at which they melt. Another significant factor in remembering the difference between the two solders is that common solders flow at temperatures below 700°F., while the hard solders flow above 800°F.

Soldering Fluxes

COMMON SOLDER. Flux is a chemical agent which prevents the formation of oxide film at the joint to be soldered during the heating process. In some instances fluxes will remove the oxide before the heating begins, but normally the worker will remove such oxides as may interfere with proper soldering.

The fluxing agents for common solder may be one of two types—corrosive or noncorrosive. Zinc chloride and ammoniac (ammonium chloride) are the common corrosive fluxes and rosin is the usual noncorrosive flux. These fluxes are commercially prepared and may be procured in a variety of forms —as a greasy paste, as a liquid, or as a powder. In addition to separate fluxes, a combined flux and solder is obtainable as a cored solder in which the flux is contained within a hollow wire; or the combination may be made up in the form of powdered solder suspended in a water-soluble flux.

These combined flux-common solder compounds should not be confused with the various "liquid solders," which are not true solders at all, but are metallic powders in a volatile cement base.

HARD SOLDER. The primary flux for hard solder is borax. Commercial fluxes are available in liquid, paste, and powdered forms, or they too may be combined with the hard solder as a thick liquid in which the powdered hard solder is suspended.

All of the hard-solder fluxes perform the same function—protect the cleaned surfaces to be joined from formation of an oxide film during the heating process. As a secondary but equally important function, the hard-solder fluxes should be active as the metal approaches the critical temperature at which the solder will flow. Many fluxes are compounded to act as precise temperature indicators, and, as such, are invaluable tools for the metalsmith. Borax, for example, changes from a whitish powder to a slightly brownish glasslike material at approximately 1400°F. This makes it an excellent indicator for hard solder.

Common Soldering

PREPARING THE WORK. For successful common soldering it is essential that the surfaces to be joined be cleaned thoroughly. This cleaning may be done chemically or mechanically. It is preferable to abrade the surfaces with a scraper or file, because one can see the bright metal and be certain that the joint is clean. The parts should be covered carefully with flux immediately after the cleaning and the soldering begun as soon as possible.

Both pieces to be joined should be heated to a temperature equal to the melting temperature of the solder. If the pieces are heated radically above this optimum heat, pits may be formed in the joint by burning out the solder or by its combining with the flux. It is particularly important that the heat, whether it be applied with a torch or with an iron, be distributed equally between the parts to be joined. Remember, the solder will flow to the "hot spot."

THE PROCESS. There are several methods by which common soldering may be accomplished effectively. The classic soldering iron (which is invariably made of copper) remains as one of the most useful tools, particularly since it has been electrified.

Soldering with an iron is dependent upon heat transference from the tip of the tool to the work. As heat is transferred, the solder will follow the stream of heat. (See Figure 235.)

A typical soldering operation with the soldering iron with common solder may follow this sequence:

1. The iron should be prepared by cleaning the surfaces. If the iron has never been used, or has the residue of solder and flux from previous use, it should be filed down to the bright metal. The exposed copper should then be swabbed or dipped in flux. Immediately after fluxing, the iron is heated with a torch or other heating device until it reaches the melting point of the solder you

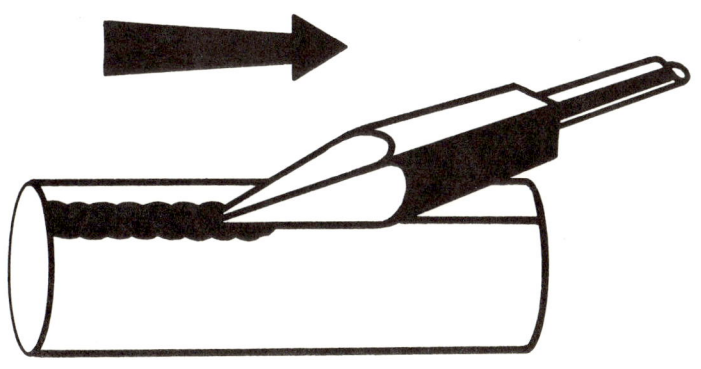

FIG. 235.

intend to use. Now pick up some solder from the bar or coil and rotate the fluxed, hot tool surfaces until the iron is uniformly coated. The iron is now "tinned" and ready for use.
2. The parts to be joined should be swabbed carefully with a suitable flux. (See the description of common-solder fluxes described earlier in this chapter.)
3. Reheat the iron and pick up as much solder as the iron will hold conveniently from the bar or coil. (See Figure 236.)
4. Place the point of the iron at one end of the joint to be joined and hold until the heat has transferred, which will permit the solder to flow. When the solder starts to flow, draw the iron slowly along the length of the join. It is well to remember that the solder will flow and the join will be made only when heat transferred from the iron to the two halves of the seam equals the melting temperature of the solder. If you find it necessary to add solder to the iron as you draw it along the seam, introduce a thin rod of solder on the top surface of the iron as you draw it along. (See Figure 237.)
5. On long joins it may be necessary to reheat the iron, but it is best if the soldering can be completed on one draw.
6. Allow the seam to cool. The cooling time varies with the volume of the joined pieces, and one should not disturb the joint until complete cooling is a certainty.
7. Remove the flux by exposing it to a stream of hot running water. If it is impossible to clean the flux off under a running stream, the excess may be wiped off with a damp cloth. It is absolutely essential that all flux—corrosive or noncorrosive—be cleaned off the joint, because fluxing agents are chemically active and may damage or discolor the parent metals.

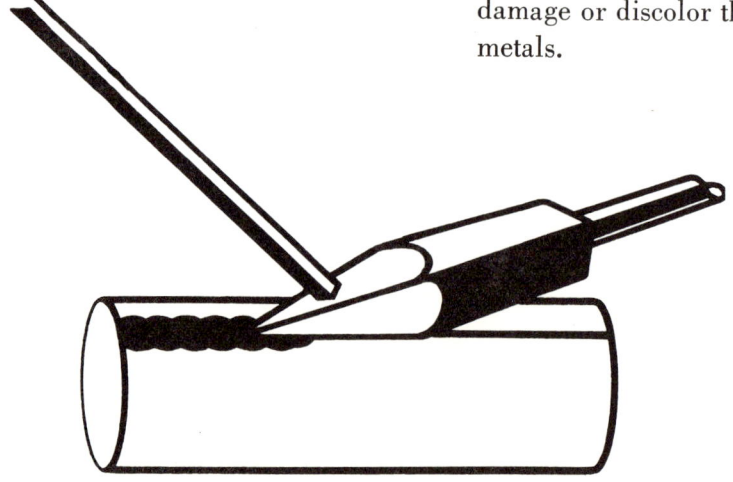

Fig. 236.

Common soldering may also be accomplished with the direct use of the flame of a torch. This method offers a greater degree of control of the solder, in that the solder is placed in position before heat is applied.

A typical common-soldering sequence using the direct flame follows:

1. Clean the parts to be joined by chemical or mechanical means as described above and again swab with flux.
2. Cut small pieces of solder from the coil or bar. (The bar of solder may be flattened by hammering it on a steel plate, which will facilitate cutting.) The small pieces of solder, called "pallions," should be about the size of a grain of rice and should be well coated with flux to facilitate placement and to assure good flowing quality.
3. The pallions are spaced evenly along the angle of the joint, or, in the case of a seam, they can be placed over the crack between the parts. A small pair of tweezers or a small brush will be useful to place the pallions.
4. Light the torch and adjust it to a soft flame. Direct the flame at one end of the seam of joint and fan it slowly from one side to the other. When the metal has been heated to the flow point of the solder, the fluxed pallions will ball up, melt, and shoot through the seam. Proceed along the joint until all the pallions have melted. If you like, the finished joint may be fanned again to assure uniformity of the flow. (See Figure 238.)
5. After the solder has cooled, remove all traces of flux.

A third method of joining with common solder that is particularly useful when attaching plates together follows this procedure:

1. Clean and swab with flux the surfaces of the plates to be joined.
3. Place fluxed pallions of solder about the size of a grain of rice about ½" apart over the surface.

Fig. 237.

3. Heat with a torch until the solder melts and runs over the surface—with one pallion running into the next and forming a film of solder of uniform thickness.
4. Clean and flux the second plate and place it over the "tinned" plate in such a manner that the film is sandwiched between the two. (See Figure 239.)
5. Apply heat with a torch, making certain that all parts of the mass receive equal attention. When you see a thin silvery line of solder all around the edges, remove the torch and allow to cool. Flush flux off, as described before. (See Figure 239.)

Additional techniques for using common solder are:

1. Wiping—A method whereby the solder is melted in a pot, poured over the fluxed metals to be joined, and then modeled to the joint with a cloth pad or a warmed spatula. This indicates the unusual plastic quality of molten common solder, which is of great convenience when the joint space is so great as to require filling as well as joining.
2. Solder bath—Small objects are frequently painted with flux, assembled, dipped into molten solder momentarily, and then withdrawn. The total surface, or at least that part immersed, is covered with solder.
3. Sweating—A gross means of joining with common solder. A pool of molten solder is built up on one piece of metal and the second piece, well tinned, is inserted into the pool and held until cool. The pool of molten solder may be contained with a dam of clay, stiff paper, or wet powdered asbestos.

Common (or soft) solder has value to the metalsmith, but, where conditions permit, the hard or silver solder should always be used.

Common solder should never be used in conjunction with precious metals, because, in addition to the

Fig. 238.

base nature which lessens the value of a precious-metal object, the chemical interaction between the tin and lead components of common solder has an extremely deleterious effect upon silver, gold, and their alloys. If, by accident or ignorance, gold and silver objects are overheated in the presence of common solders, the resultant damage can be repaired only by laboriously cutting or scraping away the affected areas and replacing them with new metal.

I once had the opportunity to repair and replace some decorative elements on a fine sterling creamer attributed to Paul Revere. In preparation for removal of the handle, which was required in the process, I very carefully scraped the joints and cut away as much of the metal as was necessary to determine that hard solder had been used. Fully satisfied that the joint was hard soldered, I applied heat to melt the solder so that the handle could be tapped away. When the handle dropped away, I found evidence of surface common-solder fusion at the upper joint. It was necessary to cut out a section of the body of the vessel and fit a new piece in its place before this handle could be replaced. It is likely that at some time the original joint had broken away and left a jagged edge of hard solder on both parts. Repair had been made by tinning the two surfaces with a lead-based alloy, clamping them in place, and subjecting the assembly to sufficient heat to form a bond. It is not unusual to find sterling vessels repaired or even originally joined with common solder, but it is obviously a bad practice and one that the competent craftsman will avoid.

Fig. 239.

CHAPTER 11

HARD SOLDERING

Preparing the Work

Hard soldering is a precise, even meticulous, technique. The silver-based alloys employed form, in a molten state, a thin, highly mobile film rather than a sluggish mass that can be drawn or pushed or modeled into place. Capillary action is marked, and this force can pull small pieces together even more tightly than they can be drawn by the jig or clamping device. A thorough understanding and intelligent use of this physical factor will produce crisp, clean joins which, in turn, will enhance the aesthetic quality of the finished piece.

It will be of interest to those metal craftsmen who submit their work to juried shows to know that the judge, after a preliminary appraisal of an object for form, function, finish, and so on, will then nearly always subject the joints to minute scrutiny. If evidence of laboriously filed or stoned seams is apparent, the piece goes out, even if it be the work of a twentieth-century Cellini!

The strength of the hard-soldered joint depends upon how well the thin film of solder fits the joint. Apparently there are conflicting theories concerning the bonding characteristics of hard solder. One authority states flatly that this is not a fusion process because the melting point of the parts being joined is not reached. A second authority concedes that the melting point is not achieved, but that the silver solder has the capacity for surface fusion. I am not equipped by training or experience to weigh the opinions.

Jigs

A soldering jig is a mechanical device to hold metal parts in place during the heating process. One mark of the competent craftsman is his ingenuity in solving the problem of holding several pieces of metal in close contact and maintaining that contact through the critical heating stages that may easily warp and twist metals out of shape. It is not at all unusual to find that the design and construction of a workable jig is much more time-consuming than the actual soldering.

Not all soldering sequences require a jig, however, and in a great many instances simple setups which depend solely upon gravity are adequate and desirable. Figure 240 illustrates such a simple "gravity jig." It would be well, in every instance, to evaluate the possibility for use of this device before constructing a complex mechanical jig.

The most useful material for making jigs is a dead soft iron wire which can be procured in a variety of wire-gauge sizes. A coarse wire of 10 gauge and a fine 22-gauge wire will be adequate for most operations. Figures 241, 242 picture iron-wire holding jigs.

The loops and kinks in the wires, as illustrated in Figures 241 and 242, perform a useful function in that they allow the parts under heat to shift slightly as expansion and contraction occur. The loops are formed in the wire before it is tightened around the vessel; the kinks are put in the straight lengths with a pair of flat-faced pliers after the ends have been twisted together.

The loops and kinks offer additional tightening advantage after the wires are in place.

A word of caution: Do not attempt to force ill-fitting joints together with the mechanical advantage of a jig or with weights such as fire bricks or asbestos blocks. Parts to be joined must fit accurately. The jig is intended only to hold position.

FIG. 240.

The Process

Successful hard soldering demands uniform clearance between the pieces to be joined. In fitting the parts it is useful to hold them firmly in contact against a strong light. If the crack of light is thin and uniform, the preparation is adequate. (Ideally, of course, the joint should fit so well that no light shines through!) The elements should be clean and free of oxides. Cleaning may be by chemical or mechanical action, but mechanical or abrasive means is best, for it offers visual assurance that the metal is free of foreign matter.

As soon as possible after the preparations described above have been completed, the assembly should be flushed with flux and the necessary holding (jig) devices put in place. Frequently it is desirable to apply flux before and after adjusting the jig.

The normal heating tool for hard soldering is a torch of any type that will raise the solder to its flow point.

The most commonly used method for relatively large hard-soldering operations, such as soldering a base to a bowl, is called the "feed-in" or "stick-feed" method. A typical feed-in hand-soldering sequence may follow this order:

1. Place the assembly to be joined with its necessary holding devices or on asbestos block. Or, better yet, put it in a rotating annealing pan filled with rock pumice. Make a final check on alignment of the two or more pieces to be joined.
2. Begin heating with a soft flame to drive off the water contained in the flux. If heat is built up too quickly, the flux will spatter and will not be in a good position to act as a heat indicator. (See section in preceding chapter on hard-solder fluxes.)
3. After the flux has been stabilized, the heat may be increased by bringing the torch closer to the work or by adjusting the flame. The heat should be directed in such a

Fig. 241.

manner that all elements to be joined will reach the flow-point temperature of the solder at the same time. Continue the heat until the flux melts and you are certain that the metal is hot enough to receive the solder. With the common metals and with sterling and gold this is a dull, glowing red state.

4. With the torch constantly moving, introduce into the joint the stick or wire, which has been previously prepared by being dipped in flux. (See Figure 243.) The solder will quickly shoot through the joint or seam and may be seen readily as a bright, thin line. Always touch the stick of solder to the angle of the joint or at the point of separation of a seam. Be careful not to drag the stick along the joint or at an angle from it. When the joint is long, it may be necessary to touch the joint several times in order to get sufficient solder in place.

5. After the solder has shot through, it may be desirable to go back over the entire length of the joint to equalize the volume of solder with the flame. This should be done immediately after the first heating process and care should be taken that the piece not be overheated.

6. Allow the piece to cool sufficiently to remove the holding devices and then plunge it into the pickle bath. (In the preceding chapter see the section describing pickle.) The retained heat will accelerate action of acid on the flux.

(Note: Soldered sterling-silver assembly should not be immersed in the acid bath [pickle] with an iron or steel jig in place if the bath is used for other metals. The presence of iron and the salts of copper in the bath will result in a thin copper deposition on the surface of the sterling [plating by immersion] that is difficult to remove and may, in subsequent heating processes, compound the fire-scale problem.)

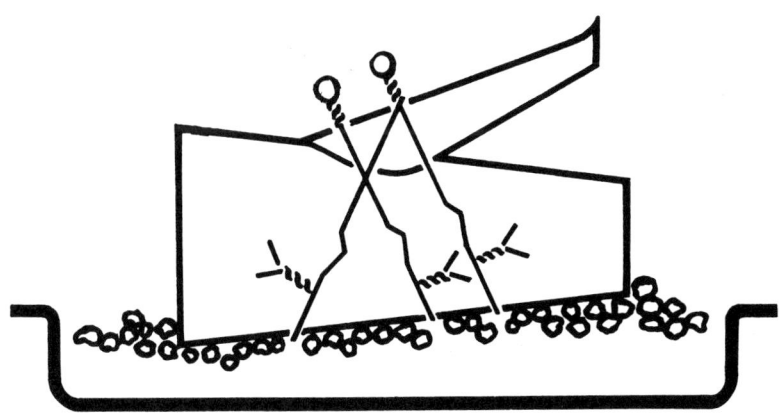

Fig. 242.

The second significant method by which hard soldering may be accomplished differs from that described above in that the solder is introduced at the join line before heating is started in the form of small pallions—cut pieces of solder. A typical procedure with pallions follows:

1. Fit the parts to be joined and adjust the jig, if necessary. Paint the joint with a thin coat of flux, using a small soft brush. Prepare the pallions by cutting tiny squares from a thin sheet of solder. The dimension of these squares will vary with the size of the job to be done—larger pieces for heavy thick metals and smaller pieces for delicate objects. With a brush dipped in flux pick up the pallions and place them carefully on the joint. They may lap the seam or, in the case of an angle, may lie in the joint.
2. With the torch apply a gentle heat, initially keeping the flame well away from the joint. The water in the flux should be driven off without undue agitation because the pallions may be thrown out of the joint. As the heat is increased the flux will boil slightly and then gradually subside and form a glassy substance that will hold the pallions in place. When this occurs, carefully examine the seam and with a pointed steel rod remove or push back into place any pallions that may have become dislodged. Increase the heat, fanning the flame between the parts. (Remember that the solder will flow to the hottest spot.) As the metal reaches the melting range of the solder, the pallions will ball up momentarily and then, drawn by capillary action, will shoot through the joint.
3. Remove the soldering jig and immerse in the acid bath to remove the flux.

While the two methods described above are the usual means of soldering in the small shop, various manufacturers have introduced solders in other forms that will, I believe, become widely used as the individual craftsmen learn of their advantages. Powdered hard-solder alloys suspended in flux and rods compounded for specific color and temperature ranges with flux coatings are extremely useful.

The soldering torch is almost always held in the hand during the soldering operation for ease in manipulation, as illustrated in Figure 244.

Another useful way of using the torch while leaving both hands free to adjust and move the work is shown in Figure 245. I have found this system to be useful when soldering chain or other small multiple assemblies that can be prepared on an asbestos block. Heat control is maintained by moving the block up and down or to the side.

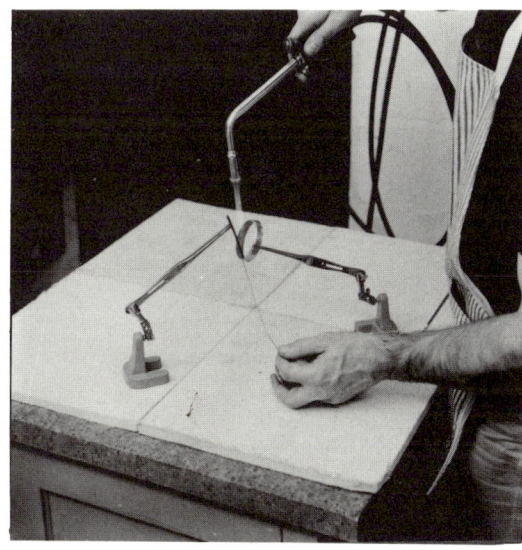

Fig. 243.

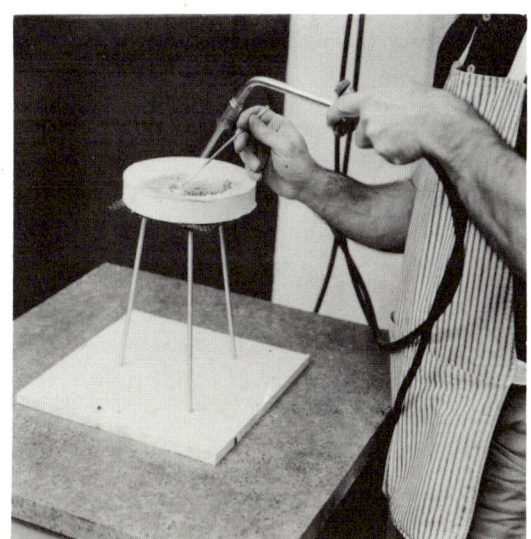

Fig. 244.

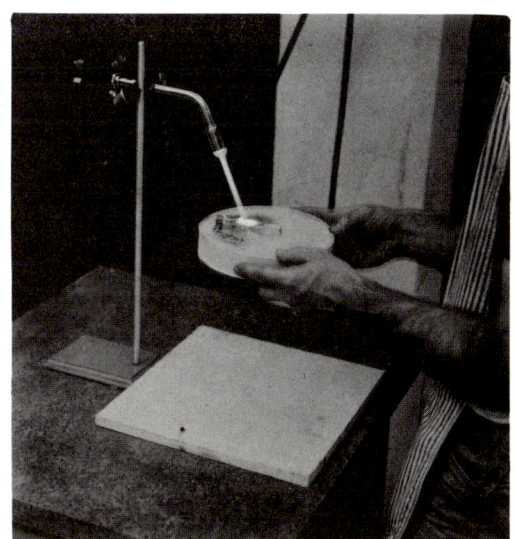

Fig. 245.

117

CHAPTER 12

RIVETING

The rivet is a simple mechanical joining device. In many joining problems it may be superior to soldering processes because distortion, discoloration, or annealing caused by heat can be eliminated.

There are two significant means of using rivets. The first of these employs a ready-made rivet and a tool called the "rivet set." The second method—blind riveting—is used when the craftsman wishes to conceal the rivet or wishes to join wood, ivory, or other material to metal. In the latter process the rivet is usually made by hand.

Riveting with the rivet set is done in the following manner:

1. Drill or punch precisely aligned holes in the two pieces of metal to be joined. It is well to use a minimum of two rivets for each join, so that one reinforces the other in overcoming swiveling or shearing actions.
2. Select a headed rivet with a diameter slightly smaller than the hole and insert it in the hole with the head down and firmly backed up against a solid surface.
3. Place the hole in the working face of the rivet set over the protruding end of the rivet and strike the other end of the set with a hammer. This will draw the two pieces of metal tightly together.
4. With a pair of diagonal or end cutters snip off the end of the rivet. The angle ground into

the outer surfaces of the cutters is designed to hold the cutting jaws at the correct distance away from the metal to leave sufficient metal for upsetting.

5. With a flat-faced hammer, strike a few light blows on the exposed and well-supported end. This upsetting should then be continued until an appreciable increase in the diameter of the rivet is noted.
6. Place the concave depression in the end of the rivet set over the upset rivet and strike a few blows to form the head.

The sequence described above is illustrated in Figure 246.

Blind riveting usually requires an especially made rivet. This is easily accomplished by cutting a length of wire or rod of the proper diameter, setting it in the jaws of a bench vise, and then upsetting the end with a flat-faced hammer to a diameter slightly larger than the original dimension. The rivet may then be used in this manner:

1. Drill well-aligned holes in the two or more elements to be joined. The holes should be slightly larger than the diameter of the rivet.
2. With a countersink, or a drill about four sizes larger than that used for the original holes, slightly enlarge the openings at both ends of the holes. These enlarged spaces will permit the rivet heads to seat flush with the surface.
3. Insert the prepared rivet with the upset head firmly against a hard surface, such as a steel block.
4. Cut off the excess metal protruding and file the cut to an even flat. One must estimate the metal needed to fill the depression and, of course, too much is better than too little.
5. With the peen or domed end of a light chasing hammer tap the metal or other material to be joined several times around the hole to "draw" the parts together and to seat the head.
6. Strike the rivet with the peen end of the hammer on both ends, alternately, until the enlarged cavity is filled. Make certain that the rivet end op-

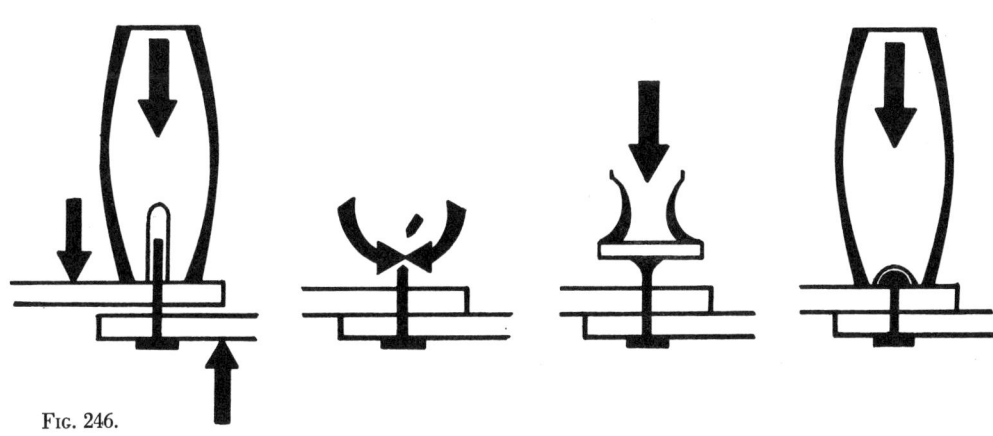

Fig. 246.

posing the worked end is always well supported against the steel block.

7. After both ends of the rivet are nearly flush with the surface and have filled the space previously drilled out, file and finish.

If the job has been done carefully, and the estimate of the excess metal left for upsetting has been correct, the rivet heads will be almost invisible after finishing. The sequence described is illustrated in Figure 247.

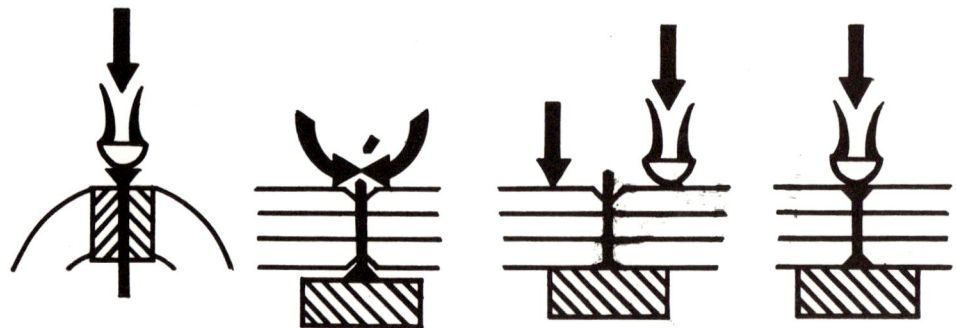

Fig. 247.

SURFACE TREATMENT

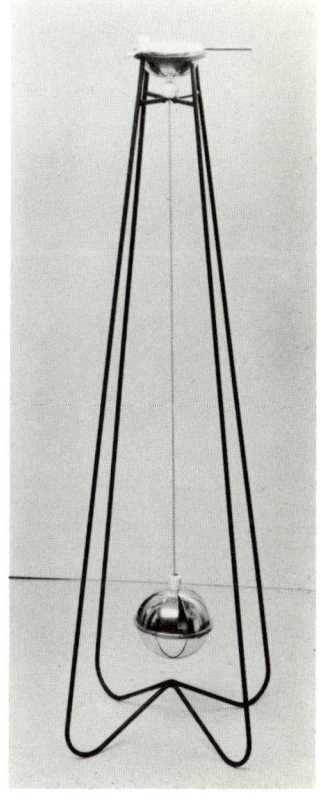

Censer, Boat, and Stand
By Ernest Toth
Brass, Sterling, Ivory, 40″
(Photograph by the Author)

CHAPTER 13

SURFACE TREATMENT

It is not my purpose to suggest or define in the following pages the full range of surface embellishments of metal which in many instances are demanding professional techniques in themselves. Chasing, engraving, carving, plating, gilding, damascening, embossing, stamping, encrusting, granulating, stone-setting, nielloing, and so on are all highly pertinent skills which may, in part, be acquired by the complete metal craftsman. An impressive and growing list of books on these and many additional fields is available to the seeker for knowledge. I would refer you to them.

My purpose, then, is to describe some common surface treatments—mechanical abrasion and simple chemical procedures—consistent with the intended scope of this book.

Filing

Filing is the initial preparation for the further refinement of metal surfaces. As a process filing imparts crispness or flowing qualities to metal objects that can be achieved in no other way. For this reason the metal craftsman should equip himself with the best tools and a genuine appreciation of their use.

The work of the file is rarely a finishing mark. In sequence, surface refinement may require many operations, each based, for full effectiveness, upon that immediately preceding. Filing, then, is the removal, smoothing, or leveling of gross surface irregularities of the raised, cast, or fabricated piece. The final surfacing is left to other agents.

THE FILE AND ITS USE. The cutting action of the file is determined by the type, depth, and number of cuts on the working surface. These factors are identified by numbers in the case of files of Swiss origin ("Swiss" now refers to type rather than country of origin) or by name. With Swiss files the coarse file is Number 00; the fine file, Number 8; with intermediate cutting faces in numerical sequence between. American files are—in order, coarse to fine—rough, bastard, second cut, smooth, and supersmooth. It is not necessary to have on hand the entire range of files. The individual will learn for himself which is best for his purpose.

Files are designed for many uses, some so specialized that the tool can be used for no other purpose. It is perhaps best to limit one's file collection to a few simple shapes and lengths. I have found that the round, half round, square, three-square knife, and equaling files to be adequate for most large filing operations. For small, intricate work these shapes are also adequate, with the addition of a few curved or riffle shapes. (The shapes refer to cross-sections of the working portion of the file.)

THE PROCESS. Filing is most efficient when the piece being worked is securely held and the stroke of the file is as long as possible and of even pressure. Resting the edge of the file on a wooden block or on a bench pin is sometimes useful.

When one is filing flat surfaces, it is useful to change directions after a plane has been cut. (See Figures 248 and 249.) This permits a visual check

FIG. 248.

of the plane, because reflected light off the exposed metal of the second cut will reveal any beveling or rounding-off in the previously cut surface.

A bench pin (see Figure 250) is a useful device for steadying small objects for filing.

A hand vise set into the V-shaped cut in the bench pin is essential for holding small objects for filing. The hand vise may be a miniature metal screw vise, as illustrated in Figure 251, or a wooden version, as illustrated in Figure 252.

While it is difficult to predict the possible uses of a file, the following treatment of a simple raised vessel is typical:

Place the open end of the vessel over a bench pin, or, if the vessel is large and deep, it may be held securely by placing it over a large wooden stake similar in size and shape to the stake upon which it was originally raised. (Do not use a metal stake for this purpose. The possibility of marring the surface of the stake is too great.)

Fig. 249.

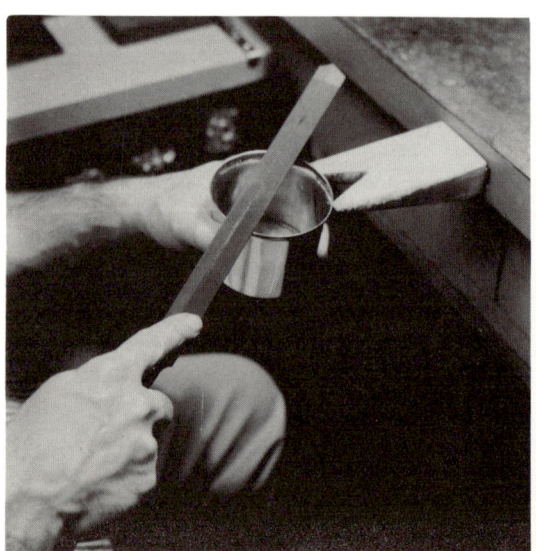

Fig. 250.

With a single-cut file of appropriate size start the stroke near the center mark and continue to the outer edge. This cutting stake should describe a shallow spiral from near the center to the edge. Continue with a light stroke, rotating the piece with the holding hand until the entire surface is uniformly abraded. Do not finish filing any one segment of the surface but, rather, work all parts evenly.

After completing one cycle, start again with a long, smooth stroke following the contour of the vessel from center to near the edge. The file should be lifted on the return; it does not cut on the back stroke. By this time you will note that the deeper surface marks are well defined, and to remove these local filing may be done. When all major imperfections have been removed, select a finer-cut file and repeat the process until the object presents a uniform surface. Filing is a cutting process preparatory to further finishing processes; so keep the file marks aligned. Do not change direction in

Fig. 251.

Fig. 252.

this case. Crosshatching of the surface can cause difficulty in succeeding operations.

Hand-Worked Abrasives

After an object or metal surface has been well filed, it may be subjected immediately to power buffing and polishing, but preliminary hand abrading frequently is desirable to reduce and align surface scratches further. This may be accomplished by the use of natural or synthetic stones, abrasive papers or cloth, or by manufactured abrasive-impregnated rubber blocks or disks.

Natural pumice in lump form (tuff) is ideal for working curved or concave surfaces, because within a short time it will wear and conform to the surface being worked. It should be used with water to flush away the waste stone and metal particles. As with the file, a definite pattern should be established, with the scratches produced running parallel.

Scotch Stone or Water-of-Ayr Stone is another useful natural abrasive and is used in the same manner as pumice stone. This produces a finer scratch than that produced by pumice and is particularly useful for local cleanup.

Most of the synthetic stones are too hard to be used directly on metal surfaces at final stages, but soft pumice-like stones are available.

Abrasive papers and cloths used directly on the surface by hand application are extremely useful because they offer, by reason of flexibility, close conformation with curved surfaces. The cloth or paper may also be tacked to sticks or small blocks of wood, to

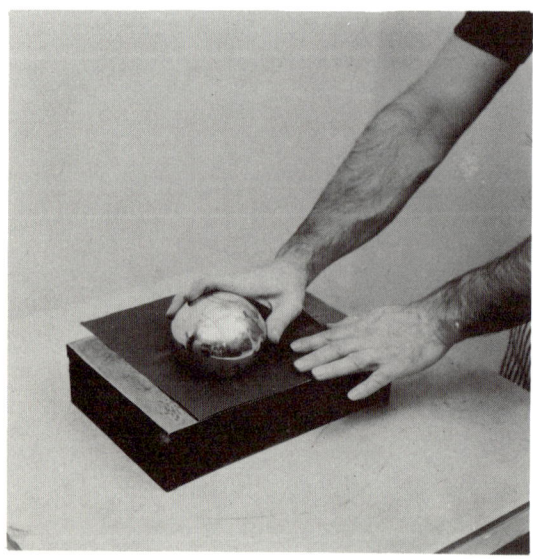

Fig. 253.

be used much as a file is used. The usual abrasive agent which is glued to the cloth or paper is natural emery (Corundum), which is graded according to its grit size, from fine to coarse —4/0, 3/0, 2/0, 1/0, 1, 1½, 2, and 3. (Grit-size equivalents are usually imprinted on the back of the paper or cloth with the above designations— 1/0-80, 2/0-100, et cetera.)

Figure 253 illustrates one use of an abrasive cloth. By placing the cloth on a steel surface plate a plane (or in this case an edge) may be trued quickly by rubbing the piece back and forth. To assure even cutting the piece should be rotated frequently.

Though not strictly a hand operation, Figure 254 indicates another tool for squaring surfaces with abrasive papers. An endless belt designed for metal-cutting fitted on a power-driven belt sander is fast and accurate.

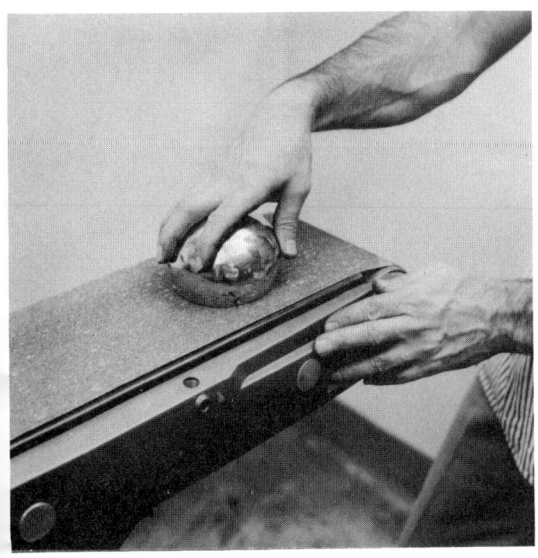

Fig. 254.

CHAPTER 14

BUFFING AND POLISHING

The two terms "buffing" and "polishing" are almost always used in tandem as one phrase. In practice the order should be reversed—polishing and buffing—because, in definition, polishing is a relatively gross operation, whereas buffing is a fine one.

As it is concerned with metal, polishing means a grinding procedure with a moving, resilient, abrasive surface to remove major surface defects.

Buffing, in metal-finishing, has to do with the final lustrous, scratch-free surface and is also brought about by a moving, resilient surface. The term "color-buffing"—a further refinement of the buffing process—means, for the individual craftsman, a final burnishing process with the use of high-speed wheels and mild abrasives. In this instance no metal is removed and the surface takes on a high luster and the true color of the metal being worked.

The Tools

For the small-shop craftsman, a direct-drive polishing lathe is essential. The lathe should have two shafts fitted with tapered spindle screws in order that buffing wheels can be quickly interchanged.

The buffing wheel will vary in size and construction, depending upon the scale of object with which one normally works. For holloware a 12" to 14" wheel is good for fast cutting; a 6" wheel, for buffing and color buffing. Of course, for smaller objects wheels smaller than 6" in diameter are preferable.

The construction and material of the wheel are significant factors in the cutting action. The wheels may be made of flannel, muslin, napped wool, felt, or chamois, and they may be sewn in squares, spirals, curved tangents, concentric circles, or parallels. They may also be assembled loosely on a center section or gathered similarly into pleats, pockets, or folds. The sewing pattern—or lack of it—will affect the wheel's capacity to hold compounds and its surface character—hard or soft.

I prefer concentrically sewn buffing wheels of muslin because the rate of wear is predictable, the compound capacity is adequate, and such buffs are readily available at low cost.

A sufficient number of buffs should be kept on hand to assure adequate application to a great variety of needs. At least one wheel should be reserved for each compound and each should be readily identified. I have found it helpful to dye the wheels for identification. This is better than marking the face, for the mark is soon obliterated.

For buffing and polishing operations over an extended period, the lathes should be equipped with dust collectors or hoods. I prefer, however, to dispense with these because they interfere with full advantage of, particularly, the larger wheels. A dust mask may be worn, and preferably *should* be worn when one is working with metals that are active chemically: copper, brass, lead, et cetera. Buffing and polishing of large objects is a dirty operation in a small shop.

The Compounds

The common and classic compounds for buffing and polishing are Tripoli (a natural abrasive, a form of amorphous silica) and Rouge (a chemically prepared iron oxide with a wide range of colors—yellow, black, brown, et cetera). Both of these may be complemented by commercially prepared compounds, some of which are prepared in water-soluble binders which greatly facilitate use and cleaning.

With experience the metalsmith will select a group of wheels and compounds best suited for his purpose. The important consideration is an understanding of the essential sequence of the treatment of metal, from filing, hand abrading, fast-cutting polishing compound to fine, high-speed buffing compounds.

The Process

The final finishing of an object is critical, for it is here that the piece reaches or approaches a state of perfection, and for the first time the craftsman really can see his work as he intended it to be.

We will assume that the preparatory stages have been satisfactorily completed and that the surface presents a uniform appearance, with all scratches running parallel. Then select an appropriate buffing wheel and dress it with compound. The compound may be applied best by turning on the machine, quickly turning it off before it gathers speed, and applying the cake to the wheel in a braking action. Then, facing the wheel, hold the piece in contact against the running face in such a manner that an edge cannot come in contact with the surface—let the wheel fall off the edge. All work should be done on about a quarter of the wheel face and that quarter should be well below center, with the rotation downward. (I once suggested to a group of students that, by comparing the wheel to a clock face and doing the work on the space between the hours of "three o'clock" and "six o'clock" when the wheel was turning clockwise, they would be using the wheel to best advantage with the least possible danger to the work or themselves. This was—and is—a sound suggestion if one's students are not so literal-minded as one sweet little old lady I recall who sat patiently until three o'clock before she would start buffing!)

In fine metal surfaces, as the work approaches completion, one may find "fish tails"—two fine lines radiating from one point. This, an excellent demonstration of surface "flowing" which produces luster, can be annoying. It is caused by a pit or fissure or an entrapped bit of grit. To remedy it go back to the hand-abrading stage and work the whole area carefully; then proceed as before.

When you are buffing and polishing, remember that the process is, until the final stage, a cutting process and that cutting can best be done parallel to the main axis of a scratch, not across it!

CHAPTER 15

CHEMICAL AGENTS

The two principal chemical agents for the metalsmith are those used for cleaning metal before, during, and after processing the piece and those used for surface coloration.

Cleaning

The chemical cleaning agent for copper and its alloys, silver and its alloys, gold and its alloys is usually an acid—sulphuric acid. Other acids—buffered sulphuric, nitric, and boric—are also used, but are of lesser importance.

In Chapter 1 the preparation and use of a sulphuric-acid pickle bath is described and in Chapter 10 chemical fluxes, which are oxide preventives, are discussed, but a more complete preparation and use description is desirable here.

As alloys containing copper are heated to annealing temperatures an oxide which clings tenaciously to the surface is formed. This surface oxide can be removed by immersion in a prepared bath of sulphuric acid and water in the proportions of 6, 8, or 10 parts water to 1 part acid. (Again, always pour the acid into the water. Reversing the order can be dangerous!) The sulphuric-acid bath will not, however, remove the oxide from sterling silver. This complex oxide persists throughout sterling-silver processing and is called "fire-scale" or "firestain."

There are several alternatives for treating fire-scale:

1. Prevent the formation by coating the object with a fluxing agent before heating it. The

flux will combine with and dissolve the oxide as it forms. The sulphuric-acid pickle will then dissolve the flux and its combined oxides upon immersion.

2. A second possibility is to immerse the finished piece (before buffing and polishing) in a cold solution of 1 part water and 1 part nitric acid. (Pour the acid into the water!) This mixture is a fast-acting corrosive and will attack soldered joints eagerly. The dipping operation is a matter of seconds. I would advise careful experimentation with scrap stock before subjecting a fine piece to this treatment. It would be well to wash the object with a good detergent or with household ammonia to remove grease or other natural acid resistants.

3. Fire-scale may be removed mechanically with abrasive papers or in the normal buffing and polishing sequence.

4. Fire-scale may also be treated by simply ignoring it! At the risk of an heretical admission, which may offend my fellows, I feel that frequently too much concern is expressed about the matter. Many objects are positively enhanced by the presence of this thin, pearl-gray, lustrous color if the scale is uniformly distributed over the surface. In some instances it is even a good practice intentionally to reintroduce the finished object of sterling to the oxidizing flame to secure even distribution of a delicate fire-scale coating.

Other methods for removal of scale are available—electro-chemical means or active corrosive chemical means—but these are not normally employed in the small shop because of initial equipment costs or essential danger in use.

Coloring

In the normal course of aging metal objects will take on surface coloration—patina. The various metals and alloys oxidize or combine with other chemicals to produce typical colors. This process may be accelerated by subjecting the finished piece to coloring compounds. It should be noted that the patina is a very thin surface coating in most instances and will permit the metal underneath to show through—lustrous if the metal was highly polished or dull if originally matte. The surface color will not, and is not intended to, hide poor surface or joining treatment.

Incidentally, the use of lacquers as protective coatings to maintain polished luster is, at best, a poor practice except in the case of monumental porous castings that have been especially treated to receive such coatings. The best way to maintain luster is by daily use or by frequent cleaning with suitable liquid or paste polish.

Before a metal object is colored, it must be cleaned thoroughly either mechanically or chemically. The contemporary household detergents are excellent for removing polishing residue and other possible resistants.

The classic coloring agent for sterling silver and copper is water and liver of sulphur (potassium sulphide). The solution is prepared by mixing a lump of the material about the size of a walnut in a quart of hot water. This solution will decompose rapidly. It is best to prepare a new solution each time it is to be used. To dip the object, attach a copper or iron wire to the piece and quickly immerse the whole thing in the prepared dip. Quickly draw it out and flush it thoroughly with hot water. Repeat the process until a blue-black color appears. The color stages will, in sequence, approximate those that appear when metal is heated. It serves no purpose to try to stop the action at any stage before the blue-black appears; the action will simply continue, but at a slower rate. I would not recommend local coloring with a brush with the liver-of-sulphur solution. This is artificial and bears no resemblance to the natural coloring process, which is merely being accelerated.

After the color has been established uniformly over the surface, it may be removed with fine pumice. Only the broad part of the hand or the ball of the thumb should be used in removing the color on sterling or copper. This approximates normal wear of the piece and is going to happen in use anyway. The piece may then be rebuffed with a firm wheel.

A bath for copper, nickel-silver, and brass which produces a similar blue-black color is made by dissolving 4 ounces of lead acetate and 8 ounces of sodium hyposulphite in a gallon of water and then bringing the solution to the boiling point. The piece may be immersed as described above until the color appears, or, if the object is large, it may be swabbed on the surface and warmed with a soft flame.

Large raised objects and castings may be colored effectively by coating them with linseed oil and then lightly fanning the surface with a soft oxidizing flame. This will result in a brownish-black surface. Wax—beeswax or petroleum derivatives—may be used in the same manner.

Much of the "mystery" of metal coloring, stupidly withheld from the student for so long, is now public property, due to the research by ethical manufacturers of metal alloys. This information is freely available through the principal sales offices of copper and brass suppliers.

TRAVELING COMMUNION SET
Sterling Silver, 2½″
Designed by the Author. Executed by William Allen
(Photograph by Harvey Croze)

GENERAL SHOP INFORMATION

The metal-craftsman's shop is difficult to define in detail. Power and hand tools, heating facilities, soldering equipment, cleaning and polishing devices, and so on are all directly dependent upon the individual requirements which positively condition selection and use.

On this and the following pages I have assembled some very general illustrations and descriptions that have been particularly useful in my own practice and which, for the most part, apply to and amplify the techniques previously described in some detail.

HEATING DEVICES

One measure of the adequacy of a shop is its capacity to heat small volumes of metal to or near its flow point. As the potential for producing heat increases, the scale of work one may do is increased in direct proportion. Natural gas or low-cost manufactured gas and compressed-air sources are safe, inexpensive producers of heat. Bottled gases, oxygen-acetylene combinations, gasoline or alcohol torches may be useful for some purposes, but they lack the versatility and simplicity of air-gas devices.

An understanding of the flame of the torch for most efficient use is of considerable importance and is almost universal in application. In Figure 255 is demonstrated the efficient use of a typical air-gas flame. The work is just beyond the tip of the outer sheath of the flame. The heat is distributed evenly through the metal by moving the flame from side to side, but not closer or farther away.

CHAPTER 16

In Figure 256, the same flame is shown too close to the work. The outer sheath is broken and the heat feathers off and is lost.

HAND TOOLS

The selection of hand tools is, again, dependent upon the intended direction of the worker. In addition to the stakes and hammers, vises, heating rigs, working-bench space, et cetera, an adequate selection of hand tools should be assembled. In Figure 257, the five major categories of hand pliers are shown in three sizes: *(from right to left)* round nose, needle nose, flat nose, side cutters, and *(in the right row from top to bottom)* end cutters, long needle nose and side cutters, and common electrician's pliers. These are adequate for most needs.

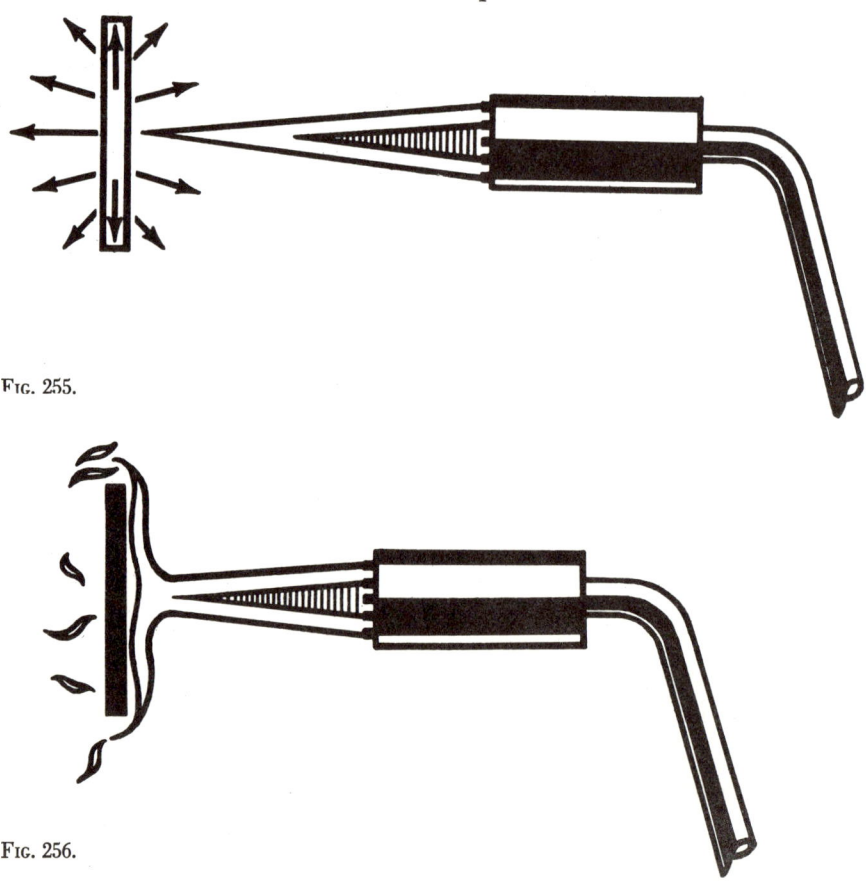

Fig. 255.

Fig. 256.

Hand saws—or jeweler's saw frames—are illustrated in several forms in Figure 258.

A common hack saw and its use is illustrated in Figure 259. The extended forefinger of the right hand is useful in guiding a straight cut.

A simple bending rig for light-rod stock is shown in use in Figures 260 and 261. It consists of two movable pins in a steel block. Mechanical advantage is gained by using the rod as a lever against the pin as a fulcrum point. It is best to cut the desired bent section from the rod after bending, so that this mechanical advantage is not lost.

An extremely useful tool for holding small objects during filing and sawing operations is demonstrated in Figures 262 and 263. The leather sling rides over a small movable lever in the bench pin, which holds the work securely when foot pressure is applied. This is a relatively new application of an ancient device.

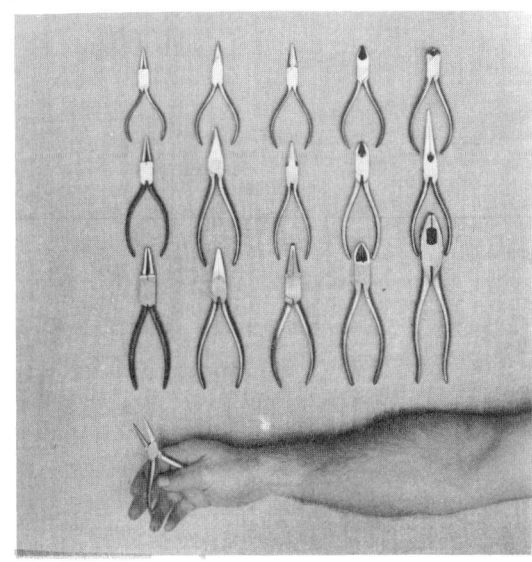

Fig. 257.

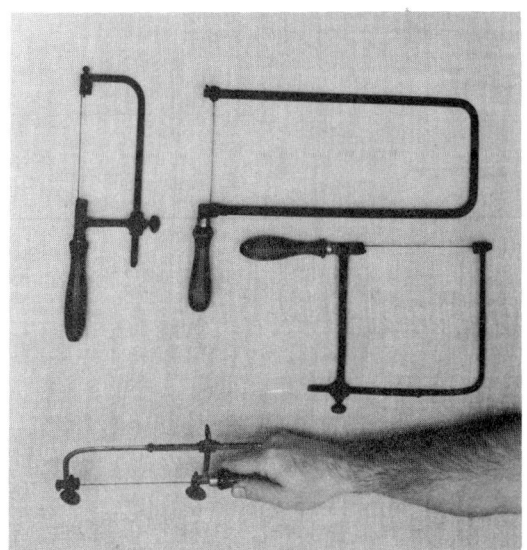

Fig. 258.

HAND OPERATED MACHINES

The hand-rolling mill (flat), illustrated in Figure 264, is of considerable value in a small shop because sheet stock and square wire can be reduced in thickness as may be required. The mill may be used also to put into working condition cast ingots produced from scrap stock, as described in Chapter 8.

A finger brake or box-and-pan brake, as illustrated in Figures 265 and 266, makes the work of bending angles in box construction a simple matter. Another type of brake without the movable fingers is called a "cornice brake."

The treadle-operated squaring shears, shown in Figure 267, is indispensable for quantity cutting of sheet stock.

POWER TOOLS
Drill Press

For versatility of use and simplicity of operation the drill press is essential

Fig. 259.

Fig. 260.

Fig. 261.

for the small shop worker. The drill press illustrated here has a milling head attached to the surface plate. This offers adjustment for precision drilling as well as the added safety of easily attached "hold-down" devices. In Figure 268, a sheet of metal is shown with "hold-downs."

In Figure 269, a surface vise holding a heavy block of metal being drilled is held in place by the easily adjusted parts of the milling head clamps.

Figures 270 and 271 illustrate two methods of centering and holding a piece of rod stock for precise drilling. In the first instance the rod is centered in a V-block made of wood (Figure 270) and in the second the rod is centered and held in the groove of the surface plate (Figure 271).

Metal Lathe

The proper use and care for a metal lathe is in itself worth years of study, for it is upon this machine that the variety of our industrial complex rests. It may be used, with its accessories,

Fig. 263.

Fig. 262.

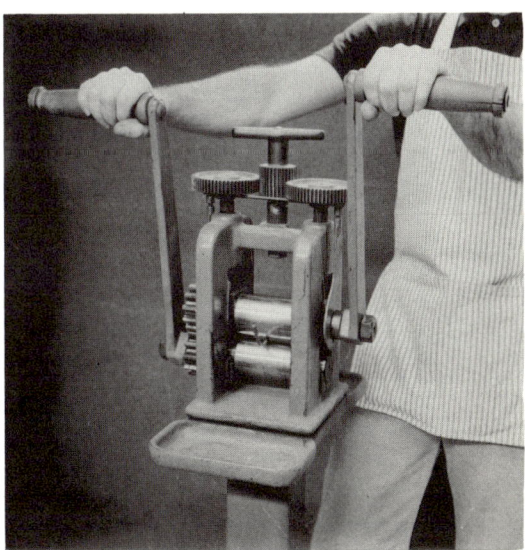

Fig. 264.

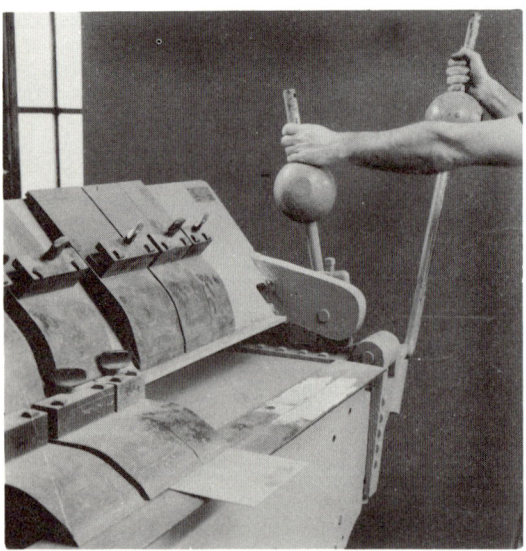

Fig. 265.

Fig. 266.

for almost any form of metal working. I would not presume to indicate the full range of its use, but wish to suggest that, as a tool, it is an excellent mechanical complement to the craftsman in the preparation of parts to be worked further by hand.

In Figure 272, a piece of ivory split from a tusk has been set into the jaws of the chuck and roughly centered. The action of the tool on the ivory is a soft shaving one, so necessary in working this brittle material. After the ivory has been shaped, it can be worked to its finished state by files and rasps.

Figure 273 illustrates another unorthodox use for the metal lathe. An aluminum rod was machined to the inside diameter of a finger ring. The rod was dipped into molten hard carving wax until a thick coat was built up. After recentering the rod in the chuck and using the tool holder as a rest, ring blanks are shown being cut into the wax surface with engraving tools. After the blanks have been formed, the rod may be heated slightly and the blanks slipped off for individual treatment and preparation for centrifugal casting.

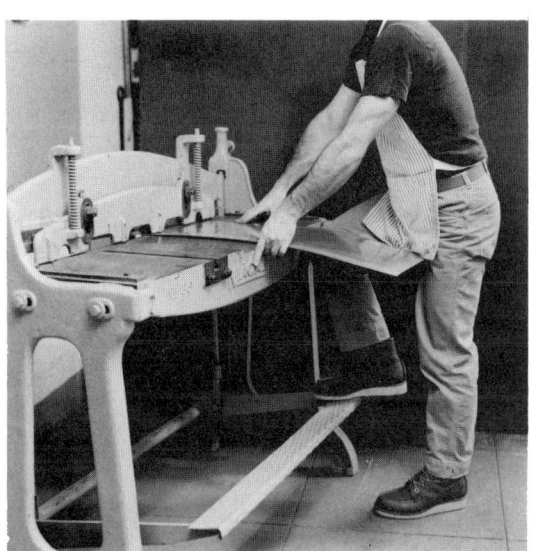

Fig. 267.

Fig. 269.

Fig. 268.

Fig. 270.

Fig. 271.

Fig. 272.

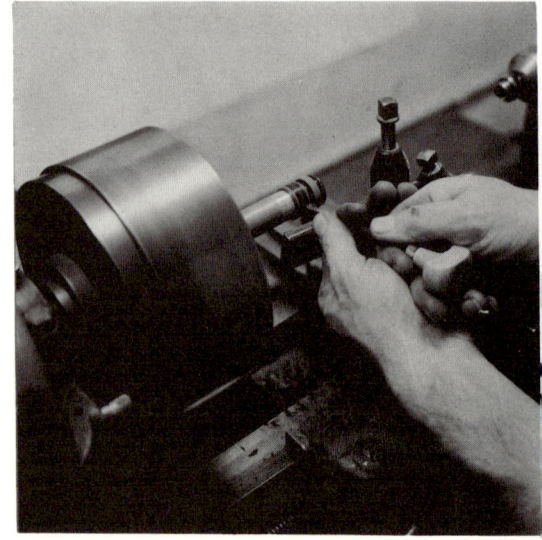

Fig. 273.

DETAIL IN FINE

CRAFTSMANSHIP

LIST OF ILLUSTRATIONS

1. Visored Salade (Helmet)—Steel
2. Parade Gorget—Sterling
3. Fluted Gauntlet—Steel
4. Etched Gauntlet—Steel
5. Ax Head—Bronze
6. Ax Head—Iron
7. Cup-hilted Rapier—Steel
8. Swept-hilt Rapier—Steel
9. Wheel Lock—Steel
10. Crucifix—Brass
11. Detail of Crucifix—Brass
12. Bishop's Cross
13. Detail of Bishop's Cross
14. Key—Steel
15. Detail of Key—Steel
16. Reclining Ram—Gilt Bronze
17. Vase—Sterling
18. Coffeepot—Sterling and Ivory
19. Goblet—Coconut Shell and Sterling
20. Creamer—Sterling and Ivory
21. Tankard—Sterling
22. Detail of Tankard
23. Detail of Tankard
24. Detail of Tankard
25. Alms Basin—Sterling
26. Detail of Alms Basin
27. Alms Basin—Sterling
28. Detail of Alms Basin
29. Tea Caddy—Sterling
30. Tobacco Box—Sterling
31. Bowl—Sterling and Wood
32. Ciborium—Sterling
33. Detail of Ciborium
34. Ciborium—Sterling
35. Coffeepot—Sterling and Ivory
36. Pole Finial—Bronze
37. Pole Finial—Bronze

1. VISORED SALADE (Helmet)—Steel
   15th Century—German
   9⅝″ Hi. 8″ Wi.

This helmet of simple, sturdy workmanship was raised from a flat sheet of metal much in the same manner that the contemporary metalsmith raises copper or sterling. The thickness of the piece—about 14g (B & S)—varies little from the crown to the edge

2. PARADE GORGET—Sterling
   17th Century—Spanish
   7¼″ Hi. 6¾″ Wi.

This device, which was worn at the throat, survived as a decorative part of military dress long after plate body armor was abandoned. The metal in this example is uniformly oxidized to a blue-black state, although it is reasonable to assume that the maker intended it to be highly polished. The piece was made by blocking out the main masses *(repoussé)* from the back while supported in pitch, and working back the detail from the front side with chasing tools. In combination, this technique is known as chasing and *repousse*. The work was further refined by carving and engraving

3. FLUTED GAUNTLET—Steel
    16th Century—Maximilian
    10″ Hi. 4″ Wi.
   An articulated gauntlet made up of twelve interlocking plates. The metal is thin (approximately 19g (B & S) but is strengthened considerably by the ridges, much as corrugation stiffens sheet metal

4. ETCHED GAUNTLET—Steel
    16th Century—Spanish
    8″ Hi. 6″ Wi.
   An articulated gauntlet etched and oxidized. Some portions retain traces of gold gilt. Etching with acid was a common method of enriching the surface of armor. It had the advantage of providing a dull matte surface which readily received oxidizing treatment or gilt. Gilding was accomplished in a variety of ways—by burnishing gold leaf onto the matte surface, or by rubbing an amalgam of mercury and finely powdered gold on the steel surface with a leather stump, or by rubbing free gold in linen ash with an oil-wetted stump. This compound was obtained by burning linen rags which had been soaked in a gold salt suspended in liquid. These methods have been almost wholly supplanted by electroplating

5. AX HEAD—Bronze
    1400–1000 B.C.—Luristan
    8½" Long   3⅝" Wi.

This piece was probably gravity-cast in a waste mold. It bears evidence of considerable working after the rough blank was cast. The hole to receive the handle was not drilled out, it appears, but was cored in the mold material

6. AX HEAD—Iron
    16th Century—Spanish
    4¾" Hi.   3¼" Wi.

A forged, pierced, and carved object. The choice and treatment of decorative elements suggests at least three design sources—Gothic-French grotesque dog and mask, primitive-African sculptured man, and Neopolitan-Italian foliate motif

150

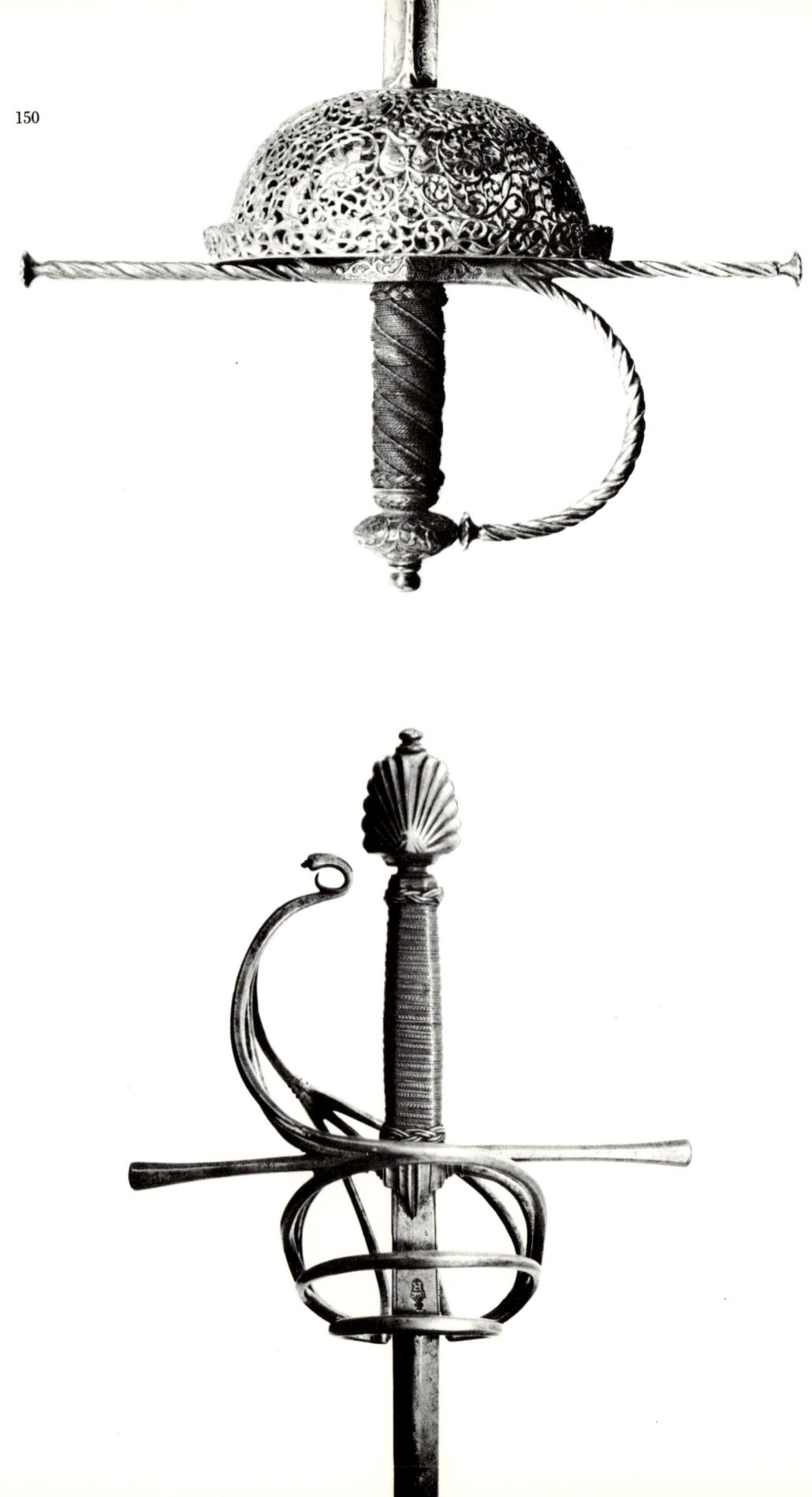

7. Cup-hilted Rapier—Steel
    Late 17th Century—Italian
    51¾" Long
An intricate and graceful design incorporating the techniques of raising, piercing, carving, forging, engraving, etching, and embossing

8. Swept-hilt Rapier—Steel
    16th Century—German
    47¾" Long
This weapon, as compared to the Italian cup-hilted rapier in the preceding illustration, is less elegant in design but is admirably adapted for its purpose. The swirling guard bears evidence of forge welding

9. Wheel Lock—Steel
    17th Century—German (?)
    10⅜" Long
A mechanical spark-producing device used to ignite a powder train leading to a powder charge in a gun. The decorative element appears to have been blocked out roughly by etching and then highly refined by direct carving and engraving. The ground is uniformly textured with matting tools to receive and hold oxidizing agents

10. CRUCIFIX—Brass
    Early 18th Century—Russian
    13¾" Hi. 7¾" Wi. ¾" Thick
Greek Orthodox crucifix, originally in the Imperial Chapel, Fedorovski Cathedral, Tsarskoye Selo

11. DETAIL OF CRUCIFIX—Brass
    Early 18th Century—Russian
A detail of the crucifix shown in the preceding illustration. A direct and vigorous example of casting. The work indicates little further refinement after casting except for embossing—direct striking of the surface with a shaped chisel-like tool, which leaves a characteristic mark

12. BISHOP'S CROSS—Carved cypress wood, gold on silver filigree, set with Ural emeralds and carnelian.
    17th Century—Russian
    7¼" Hi. 4¼" Wi.
    This cross is contained in a box made of a leather-bound Greek Orthodox Bible (not shown). It was originally in the quarters of Nicholai II, Alexander Palace, Tsarskoye, Selo
13. DETAIL OF BISHOP'S CROSS
    17th Century—Russian
    In detail, this is a fine example of relatively crude work contributing to a pleasing total effect. *(See preceding illustration.)* The stones are not symmetrically cut, the filigree is inaccurate, the embossing marks on the birds are misplaced, the frames for the carving are not square—yet the object is wholly pleasing and satisfactory

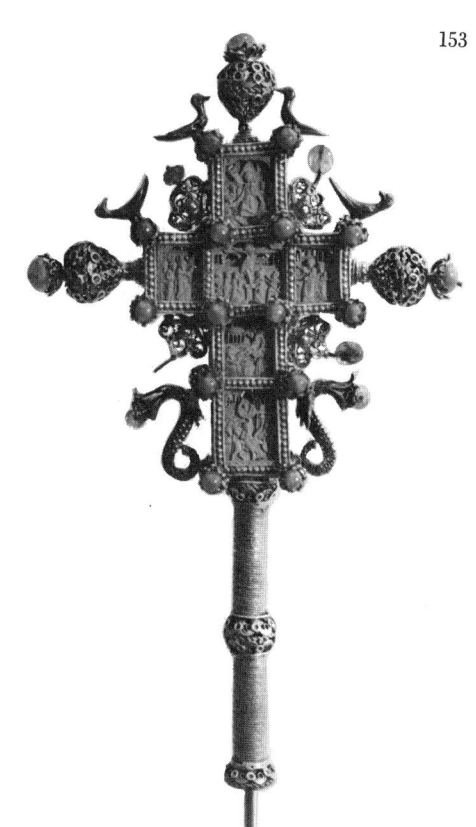

14. KEY—Steel
    16th Century—French
    5⅜″ Hi. 2¼″ Wi.
  A beautifully wrought, pierced, and carved object. The shaft of the key is hollow and in section forms a fleur-de-lis. There is no evidence of joining—a fact which suggests that the entire piece was cut from one billet
15. DETAIL OF KEY—Steel
    (See preceding note.)

16. RECLINING RAM—Gilt Bronze
    17th Century—Chinese
    2½″ Hi. 3″ Wi. 4½″ Long
    The highly stylized treatment of the wool and the detail brought about by carving and engraving of other parts suggest that the craftsman was content with a rough casting in preparation for later refinement

17. VASE—Sterling
    20th Century—English
    9" Hi. 3⅞" Di.
    (Made by Omar Ramsden)
    This object is joined at the two places marked by decorative twisted wire. The three elements making up the cylinder are seamless; this indicates that the parts were raised and the bottoms cut out to permit working from both ends
18. COFFEEPOT—Sterling and Ivory
    20th Century—Danish
    (Made by Georg Jensen)
    Jensen's work invariably reflects a direct and simple solution. The vessel shown here serves its purpose admirably. The techniques employed in its fabrication are apparent on examination. The marks of the tools, the finishing processes, the various processes and methods employed are all easily understood. As a matter of interest, fire-scale, a natural product of heating, was not removed in this instance

19. GOBLET—Coconut Shell and Sterling
    Late 17th Century—English
    5⅞" Hi. 3¼" Di.
    (Made by Francis Garthorne about 1688–89)
    At the time this goblet was made, coconut shells and other similar materials—exotic woods, shells, fish scales, sea-animal teeth, rare or unusual forms of minerals, fossil ivory, and so on—were incorporated into the designs of metalworkers because these things were intriguing in color, form, and texture—and they were difficult to obtain

20. CREAMER—Sterling and Ivory
    20th Century—Danish
    4½" Hi.
    (Designed by Johan Rohde for Georg Jensen)
    An interesting correlation of handle, body, and spout. The decorative element around the base lends visual weight in an effective counterbalance to handle and spout—a factor often neglected

21. TANKARD—Sterling
    20th Century—Norway
    (Made by M. Moller, Trondhjem)
    This is an excellent technical example of chasing and *repoussé*. The handle was cast, carved, and embossed. The finial on the cover was cast and carved. The vessel was raised in five sections and joined after embellishment of the parts
22. DETAIL OF TANKARD
23. DETAIL OF TANKARD
24. DETAIL OF TANKARD

25. ALMS BASIN—Sterling
    20th Century—English
    2⅛″ Hi. 14½″ Di.
    (Designed by Eric Gill. Made by H. G. Murphy. Engraved by G. T. Friend)
    In addition to being a pleasing and effective alms basin, this vessel demonstrates the results that may be attained by pooling specialized skills and knowledge

26. DETAIL OF ALMS BASIN—Engraved Lines on Sterling

27. ALMS BASIN—Sterling
    20th Century—American
    2½" Hi. 15¾" Di.
    (Designed and made by George Germer)
    A masterful example of classic chasing and *repousse* technique. The piece is unusual in that the decorative elements are in very high relief—the center lamb and banner device is raised, in portions, to nearly half an inch

28. DETAIL OF ALMS BASIN
    It will be noted that engraved lines are used to define and further delineate the chased design

29. TEA CADDY—Sterling
    20th Century—Swedish
    3½" Hi. 5 9/16" Square
    (Designed by Eric Fleming. Made by Atelje Borgila)
    A pleasing example of metal fabrication—construction from flat stock. The side surfaces are decorated with a matting tool and an embossing tool that was probably especially devised to emboss the repeated line design

30. TOBACCO BOX—Sterling
    20th Century—Danish
    5⅞" Hi. 4" Wi.
    (Designed by Kay Fisker. Made by A. Michelsen)
    An excellent example of fabrication—building up from sheet. This piece contains, by count, one hundred and seventy-one elements composed into a unified form

31. Bowl—Sterling and Wood
    20th Century—English
    2¾″ Hi. 4⅝″ Di.
 The raised base and lip are attached by concealed rivets and pins. The lip of the wooden bowl is completely encased in metal—an important consideration for ease in joining and cleaning

32. Ciborium—Sterling (or fine silver?)
     18th Century—Russian
     14¼" Hi. 4½" Di.
   An interesting, if overly ornate, example of a combination of techniques. The metal is very thin and the object is remarkably light in weight, but because of the radical direction changes within the form section, it is strong and rigid

33. Detail of Ciborium
   This detail—a casting which serves as a finial on the cover of the ciborium previously illustrated—may have been replaced because it is so crudely made as to be inconsistent with other castings on the same piece

34. Ciborium—Sterling (or fine silver?)
     18th Century—Russian
     13½" Hi. 4½" Di.
   As compared with the similar ciborium illustrated in this series, this vessel exhibits superior craftsmanship. The use of wire in combination with flat curled stock in the finial and at the base of the containing cup is strangely complementary, visually and in holding. The object is gilded inside and out with a rich yellow gold

166

35. COFFEEPOT—Sterling and Ivory
    20th Century—American
    9⅜" Hi. 3½" Di.
    (Designed and made by Arthur J. Stone)
    A classic form distinguished by classic craftsmanship
36. POLE FINIAL—Bronze
    Chinese (Shang Dynasty?)
    8¼" Hi. 3½" Wi.
    This device, made to cap a staff or pole, is particularly interesting because of the manner in which the maker combined hollow forms and flat sheet. The body of the creature is hollow and contains a metal ball which produces a hollow rattling sound when shaken
37. POLE FINIAL—Bronze

BIBLIOGRAPHY

Cuzner, Bernard: *A Silversmith's Manual*, London, W. A. G. Press Ltd., 1949.

Gee, George E.: *Goldsmith's Handbook*, London, Technical Press, Ltd., 1936.

Gee, George E.: *Silversmith's Handbook*, London, Crosley, Lockwood and Son, 1921.

Maryon, Herbert: *Metalwork and Enameling*, New York, Dover Publications, Inc., 1955.

Pruden, Dunstan: *Silversmithing, Its Principle and Practice in the Small Workshop*, Sussex, St. Dominics Press, 1933.

Thatcher, Edward: *Simple Soldering, Both Hard and Soft*, New York, Engineers Bookshop, 1910.

Wilson, Henry: *Silverwork and Jewelry*, London, New York, Pitman Publishing Co., 1902.

Winebrenner, Kenneth: *Jewelry Making as an Art Expression*, Scranton, Laurel Publications, 1953.

Unpublished theses by graduates of the Cranbrook Academy of Art. Cranbrook Academy of Art Library, Bloomfield Hills, Michigan.

Allen, William A.: *Jigging for Soldering*, 1952 (BFA).

Allen, William A.: *Hand Metalforming with Basic Spun Shapes*.

Copeland, Lawrence G.: *Fabrication of Silver Holloware*, 1951.

Etherington, Lois: *Repoussé and Chasing*, 1957.

Fanzini, Nancy Fisher: *Decorative and Functional Aspects of Enameled Finger Rings*, 1957.

Hayes, Larrie: *Jewelry Design by Derivitive Methods*, 1956.

Hoffman, Richard A.: *Decorative Plastic-embedded Objects in Relation to Metal*, 1957.

Krentzin, Earl: *Centrifugal Casting of Hollow Objects*, 1955.

Lawson, Gordon: *Form in Silver*, 1950.

MacNeil, Vernon: *Mold Making as It Pertains to Jewelry Manufacture*, 1956.

Milbrath, Harold: *Metalsmithing Shop Practice*, 1950.

Sandlin, Margaret Whitehurst: *Raising Metal Holloware*, 1952.

TARANTINO, PAUL A.: *Metalworking Techniques*, 1956.

TOMBERLIN, ROBERT W.: *Basic Requirements for the Metal Shop in a School of Art*, 1950.

TOTH, ERNEST: *Machines for the Metalsmith*, 1953.

WORRALL, HELEN: *Modification of Enameled Surfaces by the Use of Additives*, 1957.

WRIGHT, DONALD: *Centrifugal Investment Casting for the Artist Craftsman*, 1958.

INDEX

Abrasive cloth, 127
Abrasive paper, 127
Abrasives, 126, 127
Acid, boric, 131
  buffered sulphuric, 131
  nitric, 131
  sulphuric, 16, 131
Alloy, 105
  eutectic, 105
Ammoniac, 106
Ammonium chloride, 106
Amorphous silica, 129
Annealing, 11
  color sequence, 15
  spot, 17
  testing, 16
Annealing pan, 114
Anvil, blacksmith's, 70
Asbestos, 94

Bench pin, 124
Blacksmith's anvil, 70
Blind riveting, 118, 119
Blocking, 34
Body mechanics, 8
Borax, 91, 106, 107
Boric acid, 131
Bouging, 25
Brake, box-and-pan, 140
  cornice, 140
  finger, 140
Buffered sulphuric acid, 131
Buffing, 128
  and polishing, the process, 129
Buffing compounds, 129
Buffing wheels, 128
Bunsen burner, 92
Burn-out, 96
Button, 98

Capillary action, 38, 112
Casting, centrifugal, 92
  cope, 83
  drag, 83
  flask, 83, 94
Casting machine, 96
Casting sand, 80, 83
Center punch, 20
Centrifugal casting, 92
Chemical agents, 131
Color buffing, 128
Color changes, 15
Coloring, 132
Common solder, 104, 105
  preparing the work, 107
  the process, 107, 109
Common solder fluxes, 106
Contour, 37, 40
Cope, 83
Corrosive flux, 106
Corundum, 127
Course, 26

Crimping, 28
Cristobalite, 94
Crucible, 97

Debubblizer, 93
Detergent, 132
Dividers, 20
Drag, 83
Drill press, 140
Ducksbill shears, 21

Edge cracks, repair, 37, 40
Emery, 127
Eutectic alloy, 105

Feed-in, 114
File, 21, 123
Files, American, 123
    Swiss, 123
Filing, 122, 123
    the process, 123
Finger brake, 140
Fire scale, 131
Fire stain, 131
Fish tails, 130
Flask, 83, 94
Fluxes, 91, 106
    common solder, 106
    corrosive, 106
    hard solder, 106
    noncorrosive, 106
Forge, welding, 103
Forging, 43
Fulcrum, 75
Furnace, burnout, 96
Fusion, surface, 112

Gauge, American Standard Wire, 17
    Brown and Sharp, 17
    Standard Drill and Wire, 17
Glycerine, 84
Gravity jig, 113

Hack saw, 139
Hammers, 46
    ball-faced, 47
    bottoming, 47
    box, 48
    chasing, 51
    collet, 49
    cross-peen, 26, 48, 49
    dome-faced, 46, 47
        forging, 48
    embossing, 46, 47
    forging, 48
    neck, 49
    planishing, 50
        oval-faced, 50
        round-faced, 50
    sinking, 47
Hand operated machines, 140
Hand rolling mill, 140
Hand tools, 138
Hand vise, 124
Hand worked abrasives, 126
Hard solder, 105, 106

Hard soldering, 112
    the process, 114
Heating devices, 137
Hold-down, 141

Ingot mold, 90
Investment, 94
Iron oxide, 129
Iron wire, 113

Jeweler's saw frame, 139
Jigs, 113, 114, 115
Joining, 103
    of metals, 101

Kerr Manufacturing Company, 94

Lathe, metal, 141
    spinning, 74
Layout, 19
Lead, raising, 39
Lead acetate, 133
Linseed oil, 133
Liver of sulphur, 133

Mallet, horn, 53
    leather-faced, raising, 52
    rawhide, 49, 50
    wood, raising, 52
Mandrel, 69
Measuring, sheet stock, 17
    wire stock, 17
Metal lathe, 141
Mold, ingot, 90

Nitric acid, 131
Noncorrosive flux, 106

Pallions, 109, 116
Patina, 132
Pickle, 115
Pickle bath, 16
Pickle pans, 16
Planishing, 25
Plaster, 93, 94
Plating by immersion, 115
Pliers, 139
Polishing, 128
Polishing compounds, 129
Polishing lathe, 128
Potassium sulphide, 133
Power tools, 140
Pressing, 30
Pumice, 126

Raising, 3
    angle, 25
    blocking, 34
    checking the work, 38
    crimping, 28
    definition, 3
    Dutch, 23
    faults, 36
    lead, 39
    pressing, 30
    sandbag, 32
    stretching, 30

Raising—(Continued)
  thickening the edge, 36
Ring, 94
  and circle shear, 21
Rivet, 118
Rivet set, 118
Rouge, 129

Sand casting, 80
Sandbag, 32
Saw frame, 139
Scotch stone, 126
Shears, ducksbill, 21
  ring and circle, 21
  squaring, 140
Sheet stock, measuring, 17
Silver brazing alloy, 105
Sinking, 4
Snarling iron, 69
Sodium hyposulphite, 133
Solder, common, 104
  easy, 106
  gold, 106
  hard, 104, 106
  medium, 106
  silver, 106
  soft, 104
Solder bath, 110
Soldering, 104
  feed-in, 114
  fluxes, 106
  hard, 112
  soft, 107
  stick feed, 114
  wiping, 110
Spinning, 73
Spinning lathe, 74
Spinning tools, 75
Sprue, 84, 87, 88, 93
Sprue former, 93
Sprue hole, 97
Sprue systems, 100
Stake, blowhorn, 70
  bottoming, 65, 71

Stake—(Continued)
  candlemold, 70
  coppersmith's square head, 66
  crane, 68
  cow's tongue, 57, 66
  extender, 65, 66
  horse, 66
  side, 60
    wood, 71
  spout, 58, 67
  T, common, 54, 55, 56
    concave, 59
  valley, 28, 59, 72
  vertical, 61
    ball, 61
    dome, 62, 70
    half-dome, 63
    spoon, 64
Stick feed, 114
Stretching, 30
Sulphuric acid, 16, 131
Surface treatment, 122
Sweat soldering, 110

Talc, 85
Tennis elbow, 9
Tongs, 16
Torch, 137
Tripoli, 129
Tuff, 126

Upsetting, 44

Water-of-Ayr stone, 126
Wax, 92
Wax model, 92
Wax tool, 92
Wax wire, performed, 92
Welding, forge, 104
Wetting agent, 93
Wire stock, measuring, 17
Work hardening, 11

Zinc chloride, 106